MW00415351

PRAISE FOR LEADERFIT

"A painter takes care of their brushes, a musician takes care of their instruments, and a carpenter takes care of their tools. Leaders must do the same and take care of one of their greatest assets—their body. This book is a guide on how to do just that. I highly recommend it."

—Dr. Dharius Daniels,
Lead Pastor of Change Church and author of *Relational Intelligence*

"As a fellow health advocate, I applaud Andrew's (or Mo, as we affectionately call him) willingness to speak into this matter. He has lived this message for much of his life and what he has to impart is rich in wisdom and practicality. He skillfully connects the dots between physical strength and leadership strength. We often forget that we are triune beings. Like it or not, how well we stand as examples of those who lead their own lives well is on display for all to see in every area of our lives. We all can benefit from what Mo has to offer as he writes from a place of understanding with a tone filled with compassion and devoid of condemnation. These pages contain the possibility for transformation and the roadmap to longevity. Let's do this."

—Colleen Rouse,
Founding Pastor of Victory Church, Atlanta, Georgia

"Pastor Mo (Andrew) challenges every leader to do the hard work of self-examination and intentional growth. In *LeaderFit*, he helps us realize the importance of connecting personal disciplines with public effectiveness, physical health with healthy spiritual leadership, and integrating a passion for wellness with an ethic of Godly stewardship. This book is a must-read for any leader who is serious about making a real difference in others' lives."

—Mike Burnette,
Lead Pastor at LifePoint Church, Clarksville, Tennessee

"In his book, *LeaderFit,* Pastor Andrew Momon gives us a powerful framework that will help any aspiring leader develop the skills necessary to meet the moment. This book is about *preparation*. Through his powerful testimony, Pastor Momon explains that high-capacity leaders are more essential than ever to meet the demands of today's challenges and opportunities. In this book, you also learn that no person is better prepared than Pastor Momon himself to deliver this message. He lends his experience as a friend, businessman, athlete, husband, Pastor, and all-around leader to us in a mighty way."

—RYAN WILSON,
CEO & Co-founder of The Gathering Spot

"My brother Andrew Momon's book, *LeaderFit*, is the perfect embodiment of the relationship between leadership and fitness. He unveils the secret that those who are fit understand better than most; fitness is an investment in your leadership, and leaders who are fit outperform leaders who are not. Ultimately, time invested in your fitness yields a high return on investment (ROI), thus *LeaderFit*."

—ODELL DICKERSON, Jr., MBA,
Chief Operating Officer of New Psalmist Baptist Church

"Andrew is a game-changing leader. I have personally seen his leadership capacity grow throughout the years, and his leadership lid continually raised. His dedication and commitment to serving others have helped make heaven bigger and the Kingdom of God better. *LeaderFit* captures his contagious approach to life and leadership, and I highly recommend it."

—GERALD BROOKS D.D., D.C.L,
Founding Pastor of Grace Church, Plano, Texas

LEADERFIT

ANDREW MOMON JR.

AVAIL

For foreign and subsidiary rights, contact the author.

Cover design by: Joe De Leon
Cover photo by: Andrew van Tilborgh

ISBN: 978-1-950718-99-3   1 2 3 4 5 6 7 8 9 10

Printed in the United States of America

This book is dedicated to my wife, Kendra Momon, and our son, Maximus. Kendra, I love you with all that I am. You are not just my wife, but my best friend. Thank you for being my greatest supporter and for not only pushing me to share my life message but for being willing to help me do it also. There is nothing we cannot accomplish when we go after it together!

FOREWORD

About four years ago, God brought Andrew into my life through a chance breakfast in Dallas, Texas, while attending a leadership conference. The moment I met him, I immediately realized there was something special about this young man and that we would somehow do something together in ministry.

First impressions are always important, and of course, it was evident that Andrew (or Mo as we call him) was in amazing shape physically, but there was more to him than just a guy who had a disciplined workout life. He also seemed to have a grasp of leadership that so impressed me that a few months later, I would ask him and his wife to help us relaunch a church in downtown Atlanta that is now called Victory Midtown.

At the beginning of our relationship, I didn't know but would later learn was that God had taken Mo and his wife Kendra through a very challenging and rigorous journey to prepare them for this unique church that God was planning. My wife and I had begun Victory Church 30 years ago in the Atlanta's suburbs, and it had become one of the most multi-cultural churches in America with over 142 nation-alities. We sensed that God was preparing to do the same thing down in the city, only this time through an African American couple. The big question at the time was would it work? Would people of other races join them in this amazing venture, and could it be possible that God was about to do something that would set a new trend in the south?

The answer was yes. Not only would they be two of the first African American pastors to lead a multi-cultural church in Atlanta but, they would also set the standard for what the future church in America will have to look like!

Whenever you take on a groundbreaking challenge, you have to be ready, as a leader, to face many obstacles. That's what this book, *LeaderFit*, is about. One of the questions Mo poses in the book is, "Am I able to respond to the challenges of life and leadership with strength and confidence when the moment requires leadership of me?" What you're about to experience as you read this book is what it takes to prepare yourself when you are called to lead through a breakthrough moment with God. Buckle up because you're about to get *LeaderFit*!

Dennis Rouse
Founding Pastor of Victory Church, Atlanta, Georgia

CONTENTS

INTRODUCTION:
WHAT IS *LEADERFIT*?

uess what? When you google the word leadership, over three billion results come up! Yes, three billion thoughts, perspectives, mindsets, and understandings emerge for a ten-letter word that has been a part of modern society since the early 1900s. I think it's safe to say that leadership remains a hot topic today. I want to take it a step further and say not only is leadership a hot topic, but in my opinion, it's also a critical attribute, characteristic, and trait that can either positively or negatively affect and effect every person, place, and perspective on the face of the earth.

One of the reasons why the subject of leadership so important is because everything we do is affected by it.

Leadership expert John Maxwell has coined the phrase, "Everything rises and falls on leadership."[1] I interpret this to mean that the person or persons leading the way can determine the heights or the limitations of growth in any situation.

Leadership can be perceived through many different lenses of analysis, discussion, perspective, and even global interpretations and understandings of the Word and world. Depending on the types of leadership to which you've been exposed, for example the trait theory of leadership as opposed to the democratic model of leadership, your mode of operation and thinking will be dictated by your prominent understanding and your way of executing leadership. Just like there are various definitions, thoughts, and over three billion google entries on leadership, there are also a lot of books, blogs, sermons, Ted Talks, inspirational quotes, and material on the subject. What I have found, however, is that a large majority of leadership resources available focus on the concept of leadership and not necessarily its day-to-day practical application. For the record, fundamentally, I don't have a problem with leadership focused on theory and leadership concepts designed to expand our understanding of the subject. It is a critical part of the discipline, particularly given that we all come from different places of understanding of this broad subject.

My critique, as it relates to solely focusing on leadership from a conceptual and theoretical perspective, is that there is a void in the literature related to providing concrete examples and case studies on leadership in action. Modern leadership studies also seem to come up short in delving into concepts of cultural leadership, intergenerational leadership, family dynamics and leadership, leading through changing times, and successful navigation and management of long-term leadership.

I write this book as an answer to my calling: to awaken the "you on the inside of you" that may be sleeping, slumbering, or skating your way through life with no real end game in sight. The coach in me wants to wake the sleeping giant inside you, activate your greatness that lies within, and stir you in the direction of truth application so that you are equipped, empowered, knowledgeable, and purposefully activated to lead. More than anything else, however, I write this book to download the 20 years of leadership experiences I've acquired, developed, and in some instances, had imparted into me to activate and inspire you to be a person who understands beyond a shadow of a doubt that you are fit to lead!

WHAT DOES IT MEAN TO BE FIT TO LEAD?

Let me ask you a few questions. In your opinion, do you possess the mental, physical, psychological, emotional, spiritual and, *yes*, physical fitness that it will require for you to exemplify leadership to yourself and others?

In moments of challenge or controversy, what is your go-to leadership posture? Are you able to respond in strength and confidence, or do you get sidetracked and stumble in your leadership ability?

How would you describe your leadership perspective and posture? Are you quick, agile, and nimble, or slow, stuck in your ways, and stiff?

To answer these questions, we must first grasp what it looks like to be fit and/or to obtain fitness. Let's take a look at some common definitions and understandings of the word fitness.

FITNESS: most notably defined as the condition of being physically fit and healthy. While this is a good baseline understanding of the word, I want to offer a few more thoughts and definitions to better grasp the term. Fitness also means the following:

- The quality of being suitable to fulfill a particular role or task.
- An organism's ability to survive and reproduce in a particular environment.

LeaderFit is the belief that there is a direct correlation between fitness and our ability to lead at our highest level of potential, output, ingenuity, and competency through repeatable, replicable, and responsible choices and decisions designed to reproduce a positive affect and effect on the environments we are entrusted to steward.

It is not a secret that many people start well in life and leadership. However, we're all intimately acquainted with those in high-level and visible leadership positions who didn't finish well. Why is it that many can start the leadership journey, but very few can endure the process and rigors of a leadership journey over time and finish well? I believe it's because most people have not been conditioned and prepared to lead for extended periods of times, tough seasons, or unpredictable and constantly changing political, economic, racial, and cultural times.

One of the many google results on leadership imparts that leadership can't be accomplished or mastered on its own. If I haven't mentioned it yet, leadership requires people; "it takes a village." By this, I mean it takes a lot of hands at work, vision casting, and organizing and mobilizing around common goals, interests, and agendas.

In a 2004 *Harvard Business Review* article titled, "Understanding Leadership," the author shared, "Leadership is the accomplishment of a goal through the direction of human assistants. The man who successfully marshals his human collaborators to achieve particular ends is a leader."[2]

I absolutely agree with the belief that leadership is about reaching goals and involving others in that process of achieving an expected end. There was another part of this article that grabbed my attention, because it speaks to the underlying premise and foundation of LeaderFit. The statement reads as follows:

"A great leader is one who can do so day after day, and year after year, in a wide variety of circumstances."

This statement speaks volumes, echoing what I perceive to be a void in the teaching, learning, and application of what it takes to lead in today's world. It brings to mind the need to really understand and embrace the power of endurance. Some may think about endurance as simple survival or merely existing for a designated period of time.

However, when I think of the word endurance, I see a correlation between mental and physical disciplines necessary to push past the place of comfort.

The Merriam-Webster Dictionary defines endurance as the ability to withstand hardship or adversity[3]. Especially: the ability to sustain a prolonged stressful effort or activity.

While it may be easy to relegate this definition to physical exertion alone, endurance is a key attribute every leader needs to embrace and exemplify. One of the challenges or areas of omission with some prevalent leadership teaching is presenting leadership as a destination instead of a process.

Did you hear that? Let me say it again. Most people view leadership as a destination—not a process! Not only is leadership a process, but it also requires continuous refinement and improvement as we grow in our effectiveness. It is my firm belief that true leadership is not accomplished in a day or a moment; rather, it's executed and proven over time. This means that we cannot simply give someone a gold stamp of leadership based on how they handle a single situation in the moment or in a controlled environment where they provide a stellar response. We must be willing to constantly watch, coach, and evaluate the residual results of those decisions as they play out over time and the leader's ability to maintain the standard that was set in that moment of response.

To lead effectively over time, day in and day out, we need to exercise a certain level of endurance that translates into Leadership Fitness. Why? The reality is that the most difficult leadership decisions usually happen after the lights, camera, and action have gone away. As such, leaders need endurance to make tough and unpopular decisions for the long-term gain rather than opt for short-term external returns that can be full of temporal praise, masking detrimental losses and pain.

Leaders need to adopt a mentality of wanting to lead well over a sustainable period instead of being the latest person celebrated for a single accomplishment. As leaders, we must desire to establish a track record of dependability so people who follow us can know that the positive character attributes they see in us today will remain consistent and can be trusted over time. In sum, as leaders, we must be committed to becoming "LeaderFit!"

Now that you have some insight into my view of fitness, let's take a quick look at what LeaderFit means to me and what I hope it will mean for you. It comes from two foundational words: leadership and fitness.

One of my core definitions of leadership comes from my wife, Kendra. In 2020, she wrote her second book entitled *Being as Leading: Your Roadmap to Shaping Culture Through Life's Disruptions*. In it, she defines leadership in a way that we both agree with and try to live out day by day. She writes, "Leadership is a mechanism of influence used to motivate, equip, and empower others positively to the achievement of a goal or outcome."[4]

LEADERFIT

With this in mind, I define LeaderFit as "the conditioned ability to positively influence, motivate, equip, and empower others to the achievement of a goal or outcome over a sustained period of time with sustaining impact."

Ask yourself the question: Are you LeaderFit?

Are you conditioned with the ability to reach your goals while helping others accomplish theirs? Are you poised and disciplined enough to not only start the journey of leadership but commit to finishing your leadership journey strong?

If you want to be able to answer that question affirmatively, this book is for you.

INTRODUCTION: WHAT IS LEADERFIT?

If you are someone who knows there is more leadership potential within yourself than you've been realizing, this book is for you.

If you want to become a leader who is conditioned for the long-game journey of effective leadership, this book is for you!

And if you have been running well on your leadership journey and need a pre-workout to launch yourself into beast mode, this book is for you, too!

Let's get LeaderFit!

CHAPTER 1:

LEADER FITNESS AS A MINDSET

"The mind is just like a muscle—the more you exercise it,
the stronger it gets and the more it can expand." [5]
–IDOWU KOYENIKAN

Every year, without fail, gyms and fitness centers worldwide eagerly anticipate turning the calendar from December 31 to January 1. Why? In general, everyone in this industry knows that January first marks the beginning of a "new" fitness journey, especially for those encouraged to do so via New Year's resolutions and fitness goals. I'm sure you've been a part of this seemingly never-ending trend.

It goes a little something like this:

Self: It's the beginning of a new year! I know people all over the world are saying to themselves, "This is going to be my year!" It's going to be my year, too! I am motivated, invigorated, and ready to conquer my fitness goals! #fitness #beastmode #letsdoit!

Is it just me, or have you found yourself doing this very thing?

We look at ourselves in a symbolic or actual mirror and begin interrogating our inner person, asking if this is the day we conquer the mountain of fitness. Is this the day I start to realize my potential? Is this the day I stop making excuses for not going after those goals that I've had for far too long? Is this the day I stop talking about what could be and take steps to actualize my #fitfam life?

While questions like these may mirror the large self-help literature section of physical and online bookstores that many of us are familiar with, I want to assure you that LeaderFit is not another "self-help" book that regurgitates the adages of "think yourself successful" or "if it has to be, it's up to me." I've written this book for an audience of one—YOU—to speak to your core, calling you higher than what you already know you could and possibly should be doing as it relates to the correlation between your leadership excellence, physical discipline, and daily habits. Additionally, LeaderFit is intended to interrogate what you say you believe while offering tools to help solidify healthy belief systems or reshape unhealthy ones in the short-term as well as long-term leadership and lifestyle goals.

I think it's important to set some parameters around expectations and provide a disclaimer of sorts. Let me state the following: Maybe it's *not* solely physical fitness around which your LeaderFit questions emerge. You could be asking yourself, "Is there more to me than what

I've been producing?" Or, "Is this the day I shed the outdated version of myself and take hold of a potential future that involves me showing up as the me that I know is possible?"

Whatever the case may be, the point I want to drive home by way of disclaimer is that we all have areas of leadership, fitness, or both that require new levels of interrogation, introspection, innovation, discipline, and daily commitment. These all have the power to not only transform the beginning of our "New Year" but can ignite our commitment to a new day that displays a new version of us which, over time, impacts everyone and every environment to which we are connected and called to impact.

LeaderFit, undoubtedly, is about leadership. However, it's not focused on or presented in the traditional way that the subject historically has been encapsulated and targeted to its readership audiences. I frame it as such because my experiences within the subject of leadership over the last 20 years have often approached or presented it more so from the vantage point of how to move and influence people focused on rallying them around a common cause, goal, objective, or outcome. While this is a crucial component of leadership, I have always been a bit more drawn to facets of leadership, personal development, and self-discipline articles, books, and podcasts that examine the internal thinking processes, traits, habits, skill sets, personality profiles, and leadership attributes of those who sit in high-level leadership seats and places of influence, authority, and decision-making.

While there are many common attributes, characteristics, and methods that successful leaders embody, I believe the most important attribute is understanding how they think. It fascinates me to see the behind-the-scenes strategic development and thinking of leaders, as it seems to shed light on their decision-making and the mindset they have developed over time that shapes the who, what, when, where, and why of their leadership. This type of innovative thinking is what separates the greatest leaders, athletes, business minds, politicians, and top-notch professionals in any field from the rest of those running in the proverbial leadership pack. The mindset of a leader coupled with the "mantle" of a leader must be one of the most important things to consider when evaluating and measuring the long-term effectiveness of leaders today. In effect, while anyone can run a 50-yard dash, how does this leader perform and maintain pace in the 5ks of life?

MINDSET MATTERS

I personally believe that the degree to which we successfully produce leadership and fitness begins and ends with our mindset.

What is our mindset? Simply stated, it's a combination of what and how you think about what you want to accomplish. I also believe that our mindsets play a significant role in how we view both leadership and fitness. If we closely associate the two and understand how they intertwine as a lifestyle methodology, then we would all see improvement in our overall productivity. However, suppose they remain disassociated and are pitted as a zero-sum game. In that case, we don't necessarily see the compounded benefits and productivity of them working in tandem to improve our overall days, weeks, months, years, and life.

As I've stated before and will repeat throughout the book, I can't shake that I believe many of us are asking ourselves if this is the day we become the leaders we were created to be. Maybe it's the coach in me that my wife says is ordained to wake the sleeping giant within; however, I hearken to the famous quote from Lao Tzu, which reads, "The journey of a thousand miles begins with one single step."[6] In order to reach a destination that seems very far away, you must do one very important thing. You have to take a step. You, me, we have to take a positive step forward!

I have lost count of the number of times I have sat down with people in ministry and the marketplace who are contemplating how to take that proverbial and literal next step. While the issue is always framed differently, subject to the person's age, race, gender, and even geography, the conversation usually goes back to a fundamental framework, self-inquiry, and confessional that usually goes a little something like this: "I know I'm not reaching my full potential, and I'm no longer comfortable settling while I watch others soar. I want to grow as a leader."

Without fail, after the "I want to grow as a leader" statement comes a question which I can now effectively anticipate: "How do I become a better leader, and what can I do today to lead well for a long time?"

Hearing this always activates my LeaderFit mindset and allows me to respond from a place of sobriety, consistency, and honesty:

"You will never become who and what you want to be until you begin!"

Generally, when I say those words, I can see an inquisitive look develop in the person's eyes. It's almost like an "I know that, bro. Is that all you got?!"

I follow that statement with, "We all must steward our MO-ments (pun intended)!" I then share that the current moment in which you're engaging becomes the prerequisite and predecessor of the one you're trying to create and step into after this moment. How you handle right now determines what will happen next.

BEGIN AGAIN: LEADERFIT

A mantra I live by is that **every day is pregnant with an opportunity to press restart and begin again**. Not only does each day present new opportunities, I believe every moment we have in life presents a fresh start to realize the potential that is seeded deep within each and every one of us. It was in one of these begin-again moments that I was hit with the powerful impression of LeaderFit and how we must practice fusing the concept of leadership and fitness to become all that God has created and called us to be in every area of life, leadership, and in the legacies we leave. We all have the latent potential within us that is waiting to be realized. The challenge and question we must ask ourselves is if we possess the leadership tools, insight, and day-to-day endurance to carry out the necessary steps to realize that potential.

One of my passion points is that I want anyone I encounter to maximize the moments, because they are gifts. As such, I want to challenge us to not leave any of our potential (latent, dormant, or actualized) on the table. I want us to do what it takes mentally, physically, and spiritually to become LeaderFit.

To become LeaderFit, a mindset shift must take place within you. Desire alone will not cause you to master the discipline and dying-to-self required to walk this out. There are a few things required of this mindset shift. First, you will have to shift from fitness being something you want to attain to an attribute you embody.

There is a *major* difference between wanting to attain fitness and actually becoming fit. To embody fitness means that you no longer see fitness as a goal with a definitive end but as a continuous process of self-discovery and improvement that teaches you something about your leadership, lifestyle, and self-discipline. By embracing this mindset, I believe you begin to look at everything in life through a different lens or filter. You develop a contagious mindset committed to a lifestyle of health, fitness, and leadership where you don't just look the part, you live it out!

You may find yourself saying things like, "I am going to represent fitness today." You may even put into action the definition of fitness we established earlier. As you put your feet on the ground each morning with your newly developed LeaderFit mindset, affirm your commitment to change by declaring this over yourself. As your LeaderFit coach, I am saying this over you, too, and cheering you on from near or far, so let's go!

LEADERFIT DECLARATION

I am equipped, suitable, and prepared to accomplish my goals for today. I carry within me the ability to be productive, and my productivity will influence those I encounter. Today, I show up as my best self, leading, serving, and producing my best efforts, best thoughts, and best actions Today, I am LeaderFit, and everything I do and say will reflect my commitment to physical, mental, and spiritual disciple, self-actualization, and excellence!

FITNESS MUST BECOME A MINDSET

For fitness to become a mindset and lifestyle, you must do what everyone who wants to enhance their fitness levels must do. You have to start where you find yourself. I hate to be the bearer of bad news, but there are no shortcuts, get-fit-quick schemes, or protein shakes you can chug. You have to put in the work! In order for fitness to become an active mindset, there isn't a supernatural osmosis promise that happens. You must put in the work! What this means is that you must take a moment and soberly assess your current state of fitness. Ask yourself the following questions:

- What do I need to change?
- Where do I need to grow?
- What do I need to know?
- Who can help me get there?
- What is my current level of discipline, endurance, focus, and commitment to seeing my goals through to completion?

The last question is crucial as we commit to improving our leadership and fitness goals. To reach lasting and successful leadership and fitness, tremendous levels of discipline, endurance, focus, and commitment are required when you feel like it and even more so when you just *aren't* motivated or feeling it at all. I sincerely want to help you reach your potential in fitness, leadership, and life. I want to see you live and lead from the place of sustainability, longevity, and legacy! If you're ready to grow, be challenged, and refine your leadership, I invite you to take this journey with me.

LET'S GET LEADERFIT!

CHAPTER 2:

FIT TO LEAD

Leadership is often considered a coveted attribute and position within society and circles of influence. Many people think they want to lead, feel like they are more qualified to do so, or even feel it is their calling in life to criticize those who lead without a clear understanding of what it takes to be an effective leader. I have been extremely privileged to witness, participate, and glean from various leadership styles through the various apprenticeships and leadership seats, positions, and posts I've been entrusted to occupy. I remember when I was a young pupil, honored to be in the room with established leaders. I will never forget when, on rare occasions, I had the privilege of being invited into the conversation to give my thoughts on issues that I was evidently not fully qualified to speak on. Still, my fresh perspective was welcomed because of its perceived added value. I also know what it is like to have the "coveted" position of being a trusted voice who paid my proverbial dues to have a seat at the table. In these leadership instances, I recall what it felt like to sit at the table because of trust equity developed over time with the seasoned stakeholder or leader.

Finally, there is also the coveted position of being the "established leader" who wields the authority and influence to guide the decisions whichever way he or she wishes based on what they think is best. Let me say that of all the leadership roles I've experienced, this is the weightiest and costliest of them all. The responsibility of this seat can be unimaginable to the one who has no actual experience here. Collectively, these experiences have yielded many positive results and benefits in both my situational and world views of leadership. As shared, what I have found throughout my multifaceted leadership journey is that most people don't really understand the weight and cost of leadership. There is often a desire to gain a position in which one has not truly counted the cost of carrying the leadership position. I can't encourage you enough to count the cost!

Dr. King is of continuing inspiration to me as I develop my personal philosophy of and understanding of leadership. In an address to an audience in Montgomery, Alabama in 1957, Dr. King said, "Life's most persistent and urgent question: What are you doing for others?" (footnote see citation below) His understanding of the constant nature of serving others has informed my personal view about the responsibility and calling of leadership, leading me to frequently say:

"Some of us who have already begun to break the silence of the night have found that the calling to speak is often a vocation of agony, but we must speak. We must speak with all the humility that is appropriate to our limited vision, but we must speak. For we are deeply in need of a new way beyond the darkness that seems so close around us."[7]

For years, his strong statement rang true to me. His call to challenge us on what to speak out on is convicting. However, the deeper call that still captures me today is his challenge to take an authoritative posture based on our conviction to want to see change enacted. It is so powerful, because it speaks to the mindset of leadership and the internal reconciliation each person must do for themselves. Many people say they want to see change, but how many are willing to pay the cost of leadership? Dr. King didn't just speak about change; he sacrificed his life to be an enactor of change.

THE COST OF LEADERSHIP

One of many indicators of the cost of leadership is to understand the principle that leadership is not formed in a day but over a lifetime of experiences, sacrifices, victories, and defeats[8]. The parallels this statement has to a life of physical fitness are undeniable. In the same way that true leadership is developed over time, a life of fitness takes shape through consistency over time.

We all know top physical health doesn't come from doing a few exercises at the gym for two hours at a time every other week. The same is true about leadership. The same model you need to follow to acquire the body, fitness goals, and health improvements you desire will require the same dedication, discipline, and focus you need to master your leadership journey. For me, there are four things both of these lifestyles require—consistency, dedication, intentionality, and practical yet measurable pace.

I believe we need to put the call to lead into perspective, as did Dr. King when speaking on the call to speak. Many have cheapened the prerequisite cost of leadership, causing some to enter into the leadership journey without a sober assessment of what it really means to say and embody the sentiments of "I want to be a leader."

I would like to humbly borrow from the inspiration of Dr. King and speak to the mindset one must have to enter into the responsibility and calling of leadership.

> *"The call of leadership is a vocation of unrelenting persistence,*
> *but we must lead. We must lead with the humility that is*
> *appropriate to impact change on the environment around us*
> *based on the inner conviction of discontent for the status quo."*
> –ANDREW MOMON JR.

This is a loaded statement, and one that sums up some very crucial principles. Let me be very clear when I say we must lead with humility. For years I have stated that humility is strength under control. There are active steps that must be considered and taken to live out this strength under control. It is the exercising, assessing, and careful deliberation of a situation that requires action. The three-step process I referenced is followed up with sober actions focused on an outcome or goal designed toward a goal or positive dividend. One significant distinction of the humility I'm referencing is that it is not action-oriented. Whereas a lot of leadership expert advice encourages natural-born leaders to take the lead based on instinct, LeaderFit leadership focuses on determining the action to take based on what's fruitful for the greater good, even if you discover that what is best takes more effort and energy.

FIT TO LEAD

Being fit to lead means you must be able to differentiate between what's permissible and what's most productive. You must also develop the ability to do the hard things instead of the most convenient things. The principle here is in order to establish the leadership fitness you want, you must show yourself able to commit to consistently doing what's best for the greater, more broad group of beneficiaries over doing what's easiest for you. Developing and committing to this type of operation in your daily life can make or break your leadership journey.

When asking the question if one is fit to lead, there are several things to consider:

- Have you counted the cost of taking a leadership position?
- Is your conviction to lead deep enough to weather the opposition that will accompany this responsibility?
- Is your internal character worthy of those you lead?
- Are you committed to seeing the process of leadership through?

Let me be clear. The notion of being fit to lead can be a complex one. There are many different views on what the standard of leadership even looks like.

To assess if we are fit to lead, we have to interrogate ourselves and those we deem as leaders or potential leaders. We must ask if we are really prepared to model and lead others to a place of significance or accomplishment of a common goal. Do we have the fortitude to commit to seeing the goal all the way through from concept to product? How are we leading those around us?

If everyone did what I do and say, utilizing the "follow the leader" leadership model, what results would that yield? It can be hard to answer these questions if the standard is based on a sliding scale or without a working definition or understanding of what it means to be fit to lead.

To answer this question, we first have to look at what it means to be fit. Earlier in the book, I shared the definition of fitness as:

- The condition of being physically fit and healthy.
- The quality of being suitable to fulfill a particular role or task.
- An organism's ability to survive and reproduce in a particular environment.

The National Academy of Sports Medicine says fitness is the condition of being physically fit and healthy and involves attributes that include but are not limited to mental acuity, cardiorespiratory endurance, muscular strength, muscular endurance, body composition, and flexibility.[9]

My definition of fitness is to be functionally strong in mind, body, and spirit. It's to be prepared to respond from a position of strength according to what the current situation requires of me, because I have prepared myself in advance.

My level of fitness allows me to accomplish my goals. My level of fitness also affects my relationships, my professional life, as well as my health. My commitment to fitness is reflected in multiple facets of life.

Physically: I am training and conditioning my body to be in optimal position to respond to the rigors of life.

Spiritually: I am training and feeding myself spiritually by creating and maintaining spiritual disciplines to grow in my convictions and beliefs.

Emotionally: I am training and disciplining myself emotionally to operate with the fortitude needed to persevere when circumstances challenge me.

Relationally: I am training myself to be intentional about building and fortifying relationships in a manner that I add value to others, and they add value to me.

Intellectually: I am training my mind to continually be in a place of growth as I challenge myself beyond my comfort zone.

FIT MINDSET

What does it mean to be fit?

In an interview with Dr. Dharius Daniels, he said to be fit means "to have optimal cardiovascular and muscular health for the season I'm in. This cardiovascular and muscular health is different at different stages of life you're in." What a great definition! When I hear that to be fit is to have optimal cardiovascular and muscular health for the season I'm in, it really resonates with me.

We must realize that every season calls for a unique response! Each season of life in which we find ourselves demands a different "flexing" and exercising of specific muscles. Let me give you a practical example. I have played and competed in many sports in my life. In college, I played two diametrically opposed sports—football and tennis. Yes, take that in.

Both of these sports required me to be in optimal shape to compete at the highest level and position myself to be successful. One of the most important lessons I learned playing two sports in college was that how I conditioned for one sport was not the same as the way I conditioned for the other. Every year would take me through rigorous training regimens that served the purpose for the particular season of sport I was entering into. In the summer, I would lift heavy weights, run sprints, and catch and throw a football. I also would eat more to ensure I had enough weight to act as insulation to take the hits that came from being a wide receiver and quarterback. This preparation served its purpose and allowed me to play at a high level while taking on the rigors of being tackled and still being agile enough to evade opponents when needed.

On the other hand, when preparing for tennis season, I was more concerned with developing my fast-twitch muscles. I needed to be able to cover shorter distances with even quicker reaction times. I worked on my flexibility and agility in ways that prepared me for situations and scenarios specific to the tennis court. The extra weight that I developed during football season was no longer relevant for the season of tennis. There is a major lesson in that statement. *Some of us have prepared ourselves for a past season of leadership that is no longer serving us in the current season we are in.* There are seasons where you need to be swift and agile and readjust on a dime to be effective. There are also seasons where you need to put your spiritual, emotional, and intellectual weight into a situation and show resilience by not giving up a position. The key to all of this is that you must recognize which season you're in. When you can recognize the season you're in, it makes it possible for you to exercise the appropriate muscles that position you for success.

The particular season you're in calls for a particular response. Fitness is being able to recognize which response is appropriate and having the ability to respond accordingly.

CHAPTER 3:

DISCIPLINE IS MY SUPERPOWER!

How much do you want what you say you want? Everyone says they want to accomplish great things until it's time to put in the work necessary to manifest that great idea or goal. The goal of losing weight seems noble, exciting, and even attainable until you must take the necessary steps to make it happen. It is not just in the area of losing weight that this gap between a good idea and realization exists. There are countless scenarios: brilliant ideas never become businesses, concepts full of depth never become books, and aspirations of becoming the next professional athlete never comes to fruition. There could be many reasons these scenarios, so packed with potential, ultimately never become anything more than dreams.

I believe most times, it comes down to one word—discipline! Yes, discipline! Discipline is defined in the Merriam-Webster Dictionary as an orderly or prescribed conduct or pattern of behavior, or to impose order upon.[10] Suppose one were to take this definition of discipline and the lack of it and put it up against my statement of why many don't accomplish their goals. In that case, I believe there is a correlation between the absence of a definitive code of conduct and a lack of success.

When someone says they want to accomplish something, it's not enough to simply have desire! If you want to accomplish anything significant, you must marry your desire with the discipline to carry it out. You must prescribe, predetermine, and set in place a plan of behavior that facilitates your stated desire. The key to accomplishing your goal is putting the plan in place, determining the course of action, and digging in and following it.

Even from a very young age, my ability to marry discipline with the goals I set has separated me from the crowd. I have never been the most overtly talented or physically gifted, but I have always been disciplined. From as far back as I can remember, discipline has been my superpower. If you were to ask those who have known me since middle school up to those who have known me for a year to name a quality that describes me, I am confident they would say something along the lines of discipline or consistency.

I can remember being 12 years old telling my father that I wanted to get stronger. He told me I would have to work at it and instructed me to start doing pushups consistently. I began by committing to doing 20 pushups every morning and every night. I started at 20 and added five more each week. Once I decided to do this, it was embedded in my mind and became a routine part of my day. I would literally roll out of bed straight into my set of pushups. I would not start my day or go to bed without doing my pushups, because I felt like if I didn't do them, I was letting myself down. From a very young age, I felt that if I made a commitment to myself and didn't keep it, I was doing myself a disservice and cheating myself. I committed to this process for a year, and by the end of that year, I was religiously doing 280 pushups in the morning and 280 pushups at night.

This is just one way that I exercise discipline. Time after time, I can recount desiring an outcome that required me to stretch. I learned then, and consider it a key principle for my life today, that there are opportunities that will only be afforded to those who are willing to do what it takes to take hold of them. I also learned that discipline is the key to maintaining those opportunities. If we are not careful, we can confuse the attainment of a particular accomplishment that may have taken some work with the embodiment of discipline. In life, there will be times when you can accomplish some really good things simply because the circumstances were optimal. However, there is a difference between being a person and leader who is disciplined and generating temporary energy or focus to accomplish short-lived outcomes.

I like to say it like this: Discipline is the divine separator between the average and the extraordinary. Anyone can accomplish something once, but can you show up time and time again in a consistent manner that yields fruit? Discipline is the great equalizer of intentions. Discipline, or lack thereof, reveals the difference between a person who senses something is a good idea versus one who believes in something enough to fully commit to it.

To be a truly effective leader, fit to lead, you must be a person of discipline and devotion. If you're going to accomplish anything significant, you have to exercise a devotion to discipline that comes out in everything you do. There must be a diligence about oneself. The practice of discipline as a leader, or the lack thereof, can make you or break you. One of the reasons we must emphasize being disciplined is because it is what sustains you when times are not ideal. Circumstances will not always, if ever, be perfectly arranged. This is what makes discipline such a valuable commodity. Most people bow out or attempt to take an easier way out when times get tough. A disciplined person, however, says, "It might not be ideal, but I'm committed to maintaining a standard of excellence in all I do!"

This type of leader embodies a diligence that is necessary to be a high-level achiever. There are a lot of average people in the world. A person who is LeaderFit says, "I don't want to be average. I want to separate from the status quo and lead." Discipline opens the door for diligence to be modeled.

One of my mentors, Pastor Gerald Brooks, said it like this. "Diligence is the ability to focus on what you need to do when you do not want to do it. It's one thing to do what you need to do, but it's another thing to keep doing what you need to do."[11] When I hear this statement, I think about how you don't accomplish significant things in leadership if you are only showing up to lead when all the conditions are favorable.

Many people see the glamour and benefits of leadership positions; it looks like a rewarding lifestyle. Those who are LeaderFit understand that effective leadership is proven in times that are mundane, uneventful, and even seemingly insignificant. One who is LeaderFit believes that even if the circumstances don't appear to be rewarding, there is still a responsibility to show up and maintain the standard. It is critical that we grasp this principle of diligence.

Let's take a look at how this principle plays out in everyday life. Most weeks, I engage in some type of physical activity 5-6 times a week. I generally exercise at the gym 4-5 times a week and play golf one of those days. Most people who follow me on social media see my exercise regimen and assume by watching me that I love to workout. The reality for me is that it is much less about the enjoyment of working out than it is about the fruit that comes from it. This fruit that I'm talking about is not just physical. Working out brings me emotional and even spiritual balance. Here are just a few of the mental and emotional benefits of exercise:

- Reduced Stress
- Better Sleep
- Increased Happiness
- Better Self Confidence
- Increased Cognitive Function
- Anxiety Alleviation
- Increased Energy
- Interpersonal Relationship Development and Strengthening.

These are major benefits of exercise, and the only way you reap them is by being diligent. Don't run past that. We have to be diligent in doing what's necessary, not what's easy or convenient.

Here's a major key we need to grasp: When It comes to diligence and discipline, it's not about feelings and convenience; it's about focus and outcomes. Many people can do good things when it feels good, and all the factors around you are lined up in your favor. The question is, can you do it when nothing is in your favor, or when you can clearly see it will be hard?

The truth of the matter is that there have been and are currently many times when I do not feel like working out in the morning. When I have these days, I very rarely succumb to this feeling of disinterest. The reason is because I do not leave the accomplishment of my goals to chance. What I mean by this is that I don't leave room for a decision to be made about what I am going to do once I get up and see how I feel. I decide before I go to sleep that when I wake up in the morning, part of how I am starting my day includes working out. I decide, and then my discipline (my pattern of behavior and the order I've established for my life) reinforces that decision with action.

Whether it's a fitness or business goal, discipline is not a feeling. It's a decision. In leadership, when you make a decision, you are making it based on the fact that you have a vision of something bigger than the feelings that may arise in moments of resistance. In essence, discipline and establishing a life led by discipline guards you against taking the easy way out.

The Bible speaks to this in Proverbs 13:12, which reads, "Hope deferred makes the heart sick, but a longing fulfilled is a tree of life" (New International Version).

When I read this scripture, I hear a message encouraging us to not allow things we say we want to accomplish to linger in the balance of our lack of commitment to accomplish those very things. As we set our eyes on a goal, it is imperative that we move forward in discipline to finish it, because if we don't, we will defer that goal and find ourselves having regret. The regret of not doing something that you know you have the ability to do can make you sick and leave you feeling like less than who you know you are capable of being. However, there is something special that happens when you exercise discipline in moving forward with your goals. You come to a place where the longing you had is now fulfilled, and you feel the life that comes from fulfilling your goals.

Discipline is a foundational ingredient to effective and high levels of leadership. In his book *Spiritual Leadership*, J. Oswald Sanders makes a very pointed and important statement about leadership, stating, "Discipline is yet another responsibility of the leader, a duty often unwelcome."[12] Discipline is not just a nice attribute that can add to your leadership; it is an ingredient that is critical and imperative for anyone who calls themselves or aspires to be a leader. The very nature of leadership is to lead others, whether from up close or afar into an improved state of being. The presence of discipline, or the lack thereof, will ultimately dictate the fruit of your leadership.

Those who we are assigned to lead will reproduce what we've modeled. This is important to say, because if you're not satisfied with your leadership results, you often don't have to look far to find where the problem is. As Michael Jackson once sang, "I'm starting with the man in the mirror." We all have to look at ourselves to analyze what we have modeled, or better yet, what we haven't modeled. We must take responsibility for the result of our leadership. There will be some people who will watch how you practice your disciplines and emulate what they see. There will be others that will watch how you practice your disciplines, and they will be convicted into correction by what they see, as you are validated by the disciplines with which you've fortified your life. To be LeaderFit means to be disciplined. As discipline becomes a more regular part of your life, I believe you will see the fruit of your life exponentially increase.

ARE YOU A DISCIPLINED LEADER?

Are you willing to go through the hard steps of pushing past convenience to accomplish your potential? Discipline separates those who say they want to do something and those who actually do what they set out to accomplish.

Here are some questions to ask yourself as you look to grow as a leader.

- In what areas do I need to grow in my discipline?
- How can I grow in discipline?
- Do my desire and my discipline levels match?
- How will I be better if I institute discipline in my life?

CHAPTER 4:

HOW'S YOUR CORE STRENGTH? (CORE VALUES)

L eadership is not simply about how you appear on the outside or in one particular moment with others. Leadership is about what you do consistently, and even more so, who you are when people are not looking. I have witnessed so many people focusing on how they *appear* to be as a leader while neglecting the most important things, which is who you actually are from your core.

Who are you when no one is looking, and what will you stand up for as a core value? Living a life committed to fitness has very strong parallels to how you will present yourself outwardly at the expense of building yourself up from the inside. Many people who are dedicated to their fitness regimens spend countless hours at the gym working out, sweating intensely.

The challenge with this is that you can be dedicated to something that's not yielding the optimal or correct results. We are clear that it's a good thing for a person to commit themselves to working out. What we may not be clear on is that you can be very committed to doing something that's not the most efficient use of your time and energy, nor is it yielding the best result.

Let me be clear in stating that demonstrating discipline is a good thing. The challenge, however, is that it is possible to be very disciplined and still find yourself lacking when it comes to leadership or your physical fitness. You might be scratching your head, saying, "I thought you said that discipline was the key to successfully becoming LeaderFit?" While discipline is a key component in becoming LeaderFit, I need to push this understanding a little further.

Looking at the parallels of the leadership journey and the fitness journey, two things are inconsistent. In both, there is a way that we show up outwardly that gives the appearance of commitment and strength, which can be very deceiving. Unfortunately, today, we generally judge the effectiveness of someone's leadership by how well they perform in front of people. However, there is a question that we must all ask as the true measure of a leader's effectiveness: "Do my core values match my outward representation?" Simply put, does what I say and do when no one is looking match my outward persona and presentation?

It is the same with fitness. We celebrate the person with the outward expression of physical fitness, the muscles, the lean physique, or even the visual image of appearing to be functionally strong. The challenge with the eye test is that you can only tell so much by looking. One of the true ways to judge physical fitness is to investigate how strong a particular part of a person's body is.

The part of the body that tells a larger story of complete fitness is a person's core. This part of the body either validates or reveals the true state of a person's fitness. "Your core is a complex series of muscles extending far beyond your abs, including everything besides your arms and legs."[13] I am asked on a regular basis about my workout routine. I routinely share that my routine is one that adopts a functional training approach, meaning my workouts are comprised of exercises that incorporate functional movements, or movements that can translate into life outside the gym.

I generally work two major muscle groups each day while ensuring that I incorporate core exercises every day. I often receive a "big eyes" emoji if I'm in a text message exchange about the subject, followed by, "Core every day?" I respond by saying, "Yes! Core every day."

If my core is strong, I can build around it as a base to ensure the rest of my body is strong. You may be wondering if this emphasis on your core is really that big of a deal. It absolutely is, and let me tell you why. Your core is incorporated in almost every movement of the human body. In essence, the core of a person's body is an essential driving force that determines the ability to perform general and specific functions. It is the strength and condition of a person's core that really speaks to their level of fitness. It reinforces opportunities for them to move and reveals the limitations that may be present based on the presence, or lack of, core strength and ability.

Whether it's in your traditional leadership or your journey of physical fitness, you have to pay attention to the state of your core. When it comes to being LeaderFit, we must intentionally assess the state of our core. If we want to reach our potential as leaders, we must spend time evaluating whether our core values are in line with what we are or want to be presenting outwardly. The state of our core (our core values) must be something we pay attention to if we are going to lead at high levels. Let's take a more detailed look at our working definition of "core values" by looking at these words individually and then together.

We have defined the core of our bodies as an essential driving force that determines the ability to perform general and specific functions. The Cambridge Dictionary defines values as the principles that help you decide what is right and wrong, and how to act in various situation.[14] To drive it home a little more, I would like to borrow from an intriguing explanation of the word by John C. Maxwell. In his book *Change Your World,* Maxwell states, "Values are principles that guide your decisions and behaviors. When those values are good, they bring only benefits—never harm—to yourself and others."[15] If we take both of these definitions and combine them, what we see is a great measure for something extremely important. I am saying that a core value is a principle that you live by that helps you decide your behavior. It is at the center of your life and determines how you will live.

This working definition relates to both fitness and leadership alike. In our leadership, it is critical that as a leader, you take time to discover your core values. One of the primary reasons this is so important is because you cannot strengthen or reinforce what you have not identified as something that needs attention. In both our leadership and fitness journeys, neglect of our core is far too common.

In a 2002 *Harvard Business Review* article, Author Patrick Lencioni speaks to the importance of values and how they affect our organizations and our personal leadership. He first spoke on how values set the pace for every leader and organization. The interesting thing is that he wasn't just saying that values are good to have for the intrinsic sake of "being good." Lencioni brought attention to the cost of being a company or person of values, saying, "Coming up with strong values and sticking to them requires real guts."[16]

I believe he is conveying that anyone can say they have values, but it takes discipline and focus to prove it. The thing about being a person or organization of values is that every decision you make, every response you give, and every step toward progress you take must be measured against what you claim to be your core values. What makes this challenging is that opportunities will consistently give you the option of compromising your stated core values.

When presented with an opportunity to compromise on a value or take the easy way out, I ask, "Do you really believe what you say you believe?" This becomes the litmus test of what's truly at your core.

The strength of our core in either leadership or fitness exposes the capacity to handle pressure. Here's a principle to live by: When your core is strong, you can push through moments of adversity while not compromising your posture. Essentially, you have to be so invested in the standard of your values that you won't let them waver despite hardships you may encounter.

This is true in leadership and fitness. I have seen first-hand how people who look strong reveal their true state of fitness when challenged. I often notice there are many people who workout a lot but may not necessarily be fit. Over time, many people have asked to join me in a workout session. While I don't mind, I do want them to come ready to work and not slow me down.

As I stated before, I incorporate core exercise in my daily workouts. When I have a workout partner, I generally start with an exercise that activates the core. This is always telling of how the training session will go. Many people start well. They begin with intensity out of the gate, looking to challenge or keep pace with me. Generally, about five minutes into the warmup, their state of fitness becomes apparent. Because my first ten minutes are generally core exercises, I start to see their posture change. Those who started moving fast and standing strong begin to bend over and place their hands on their knees.

What I'm saying is that anyone can start well and begin the journey of leadership with the right posture. What's really important is how you will stand when you are tested at your core. The challenging thing about committing to your core values is that they expose weak areas of conviction. As Lencioni said, "Sticking with your values takes guts." It takes guts, because it's always easier to relax your standards. When you do so, however, you are cheating yourself. If you don't hold to the values you've established, you forfeit what you know is right for what feels good in the moment. People often tell me that I get in a zone when I'm at the gym. They say they admire my work ethic and the ability to discipline myself to workout and train my body the way I do. Many of them ask what I'm training for. My answer is always the same; I look them right in the eye with extreme confidence and say, "I'm training for life!"

When I say that, I generally will observe a puzzled look that quickly shifts into a look of revelation and comprehension. I follow it up by explaining how I always want to be ready for whatever life presents, meaning I put myself in position to strengthen my core when working out so that I can maintain a posture of strength as I lead. There are principles that I live by that allow me to establish my core values and remain committed to them. Here are a few:

- Decide your non-negotiables.
  - You can't build what you haven't identified.
  - Evaluate what's important to you at your core.
- Commit to reinforcing your core values.
  - Decide that when your core values are challenged, you will not compromise.
  - Remain aware that you will encounter challenges and decide ahead of time that you will not waiver.
- Exercise your core daily.
  - Spend time practicing behaviors that are in line with your core values.
  - Put yourself in situations that will build your core values.

Your core values will inevitably be tested. Therefore, you must decide long before the challenge comes where you will stand.

I often say, "Commit to finishing before you start." This is an affirmation that I will not compromise my core-value standards. I commit myself to only accepting and perpetuating actions that coincide with what I've identified as central to my belief systems.

How strong is your core, and what are you doing to exercise it daily?

CHAPTER 5:

THE STRONG SURVIVE?

e've all heard the saying, "Only the strong survive," right? In the context of LeaderFit, I want us to dive deeper and unpack this further. When I examine the attributes of those who've committed to being LeaderFit, they possess a unique set of attributes that are a part of their spiritual, physical, mental, and interpersonal wirings. Each of these different areas requires a deliberate and unique focus to build the strength to lead in an effective, progressive way.

Strength is often categorized as a visible outward display. The word strong is traditionally defined as being marked by having physical, moral, or intellectual power. Another definition of being strong is something or someone who moves with rapidity or in a forceful manner. While these are accurate definitions of what it means to be strong, they are not all-encompassing.

A person who strives to be LeaderFit focuses not only on being strong in the ways that show up in the exertion of outward force. A person who is LeaderFit builds their spiritual, physical, mental, and interpersonal strength as well.

STRENGTH BUILDING

SPIRITUAL STRENGTH

As those who ascribe to spiritual leadership, we have to ensure that we are not leaning more on our natural abilities than on God's spiritual ability. There must be a dependence on God through Jesus as the greater One who gives us the ability to persevere, conquer, and lead at high levels.

The Bible says in Ephesians 6:12, "For our struggle is not against flesh and blood, but against the rulers, against the authorities, against the powers of this dark world and against the spiritual forces of evil in the heavenly realms" (NIV).

Part of the understanding we gain when we read this scripture is that neither our leadership nor our success is based on what we can do naturally. As those who are growing in our leadership ability, we must build this muscle by practicing the dependence on the spiritual over the natural. We must consciously submit our plans and preferences to God's leadership over what we could do based on our own intellect, feelings, or even past modes of operation.

A key to building our spiritual strength is implementing spiritual disciplines that will support the desire to build this area of our lives. What are the things that you are doing to develop your spiritual strength? For some, it might be that you need to commit to reading your Bible daily, along with supplemental material that builds your spiritual awareness. Others may need to pursue intentional relationships with individuals who are committed to building themselves spiritually so that you can have accountability in your growth. This is so important, because many times, we cannot see our areas of growth opportunity until we have a person to challenge us in our current state of living.

PHYSICAL STRENGTH

While it may seem like an obvious area of emphasis for this journey, physical strength takes focus and intentionality to develop. The first thing to understand is that building physical strength means you have to push past your current level of strength and output.

In a 2015 article titled, "Building Strength," Tim Henriques shares tips about how to build strength. He says, "Strength isn't that hard to build."[17]

Upon reading that, some of you immediately ask yourself, "Well, what's wrong with me?" He clarifies that statement, saying what he really means is that it's not that "complicated," though it is difficult because it takes a lot of effort, time, and discipline. He shares some quick tips that I think help us build our physical strength and impact our leadership journey outside of the gym.

- **Exercise selection:** Selecting the appropriate exercises is critical, because time spent on movements that won't help you achieve your personal goals is wasted time. As a leader, this is also a crucial point. One of the worst things you can do is utilize your sweat equity on the wrong output, which will not yield the results you're looking for.

- **Proper form:** This is a close runner-up to exercise selection. It is critical to take the time to learn proper form, because without it, you set yourself up for injury. I like to say it like this: Proper form prevents pain. What I mean is that both in physical exercise and leadership, when you properly position yourself for the action you are going to take, you have a better chance of getting the maximum benefit. When you don't establish the foundation or the correct form, you set yourself up for hurt and pain by omitting key factors in your leadership.

- **Follow progressive overload**: In simple terms, you have to challenge yourself to do more than you could before. No one grows by doing the same thing over and over again. To increase your physical fitness, you have to push yourself and challenge your previous limitations. It is the same in your leadership. You have to constantly put yourself in positions to take on new challenges that stretch the understanding of what you thought you knew. This doesn't mean that you put yourself in unreasonable scenarios that are many levels beyond your leadership capability. What it means is that you become diligent about adding a little more weight at a time. At the gym, this would look like adding five or ten pounds at a time, incrementally, growing in your ability to lift your new normal. What you are doing is stretching and shocking both your physical and leadership muscles so that you are increasing your capacity to lift and handle more.

■ **Allow full recovery between working sets**: When building physical strength, rest is just as important, and sometimes more important, than the activity you're trying to complete. You have to know when to take a step back in order to have the energy to engage in what's necessary for you to grow. Too many leaders exert extreme amounts of energy and feel like they have or need to keep pushing without taking time to recover, reflect, and restart. I would like to share this principle with all the go-getters and people who feel they can never stop and don't stop. While it is great that you are determined to push yourself, there are times when pushing without proper consideration could do more harm than good. I want to encourage you to be comfortable with taking more time to recover so that you can truly reap the benefit of your exercise.

This is applicable in both physical fitness and leadership. It is better to take a little longer to refresh for the sake of where you are going instead of disqualifying yourself because of lack of wisdom at the moment. This is key to understand, because pushing through at the expense of executing at your full potential is actually counterproductive. If you're like me, you don't want to work against yourself. And that's what happens when you don't employ this principle.

■ **Set high goals for yourself**: In order to build strength, you have to exercise what I call breakthrough mentality. The breakthrough mentality says that in order to grow, build, and progress beyond your current state, you need to first assess where you are. After assessing where you are, you need to set a goal that will exceed that place so that you can go to the next level. Once you've accomplished this, you now can begin the process of setting your mind on going after that goal with focus and intensity. Here is where the breakthrough begins to happen; you have to believe that you can not only make it to the goal, but push past the goal. The challenge most people have is that they don't set goals at all, and if they do, they are goals that don't challenge them. When you set high goals for yourself, you're testing your resilience as well as your ability to stretch past your comfort zone. There's an old saying that states that the only thing that lives in a comfort zone is comfort. That's why so many people live in comfort and don't build strength, because it's easy to remain average, but it takes intentionality to break through what used to be a limitation.

- **Avoid excessive variation with your training programs**: In both leadership and fitness, this principle is key. Many people find themselves investing hours and even years in their leadership and fitness journeys, wondering why they are not seeing progress. They are putting in the time and energy, so what's the problem? The problem is that they never pick a path and stick with it. In leadership, this is a boss or supervisor who is always shifting in the wind of their leadership approach based on the latest fad they read about in a leadership magazine. The same is true for the person on their fitness journey who is subscribed to 12 random YouTube channels on health and fitness but never picks one and commits to seeing it through. The bottom line of this principle is this: Be consistent. You will never see sustainable and measurable progress if you constantly switch your approach without giving your chosen path time to materialize and bear fruit. If you want to see change, you must commit to a direction and work it until you have truly put in the effort to yield the expected result.

MENTAL STRENGTH

Mental strength is vitally important to both our leadership and fitness journeys. The level of your mental strength can absolutely make you or break you. This is the area that truly separates those who are LeaderFit and those who simply sit. Just like overall leadership skills,

LEADERFIT | YOUR PERSONAL GUIDE TO LEADERSHIP LONGEVITY

mental strength is something that can be developed through intentionality and focus. In a 2013 *Forbes Magazine* article, contributing writer and psychotherapist Amy Morin writes in depth about ways to increase your mental strength. She starts off by describing what she believes mental strength to be. "To me, mental strength means that you regulate your emotions, manage your thoughts, and behave in a positive manner, despite your circumstances. Developing mental strength is about finding the courage to live according to your values and being bold enough to create your own definition of success."[18]

I love this definition, because I, too, believe that mental strength connotes one's ability to not be led by how you feel, but lead by what you sincerely believe. The reality is that often, circumstances will rarely be ideal enough for you to accomplish anything of note. If we allowed ourselves to be dependent on favorable circumstances to do anything significant, very few things worth talking about would be accomplished. I also agree that mental toughness is about both having and living with courage in a way that audibly and intrinsically speaks to your commitment to your core values as we talked about in the last chapter.

Morin lists a few exercises that can help you develop mental strength.

■ **Evaluate your core beliefs:** We've taken time to discuss the importance of building and focusing on our core values. Morin also states that it's important to identify and then evaluate your core beliefs. This is important when building mental strength because of the implications of those beliefs on your life. There could be some areas within those beliefs that could use some intentional modifying if they are not positively serving you.

- **Expend your mental energy wisely:** Many people spend precious energy and brainpower focusing more on things they cannot control than on what they can. Morin encourages us to save mental energy on productive tasks and things that will yield a high R.O.E (Return on Energy). Practicing the art of directing your energy will yield tremendous dividends.

- **Replace negative thoughts with productive thoughts:** We first have to become conscious of how we are thinking in order to begin to separate the positive thoughts from the negative ones. Many of us don't realize how much we bend toward negative thoughts. Taking the time to identify the origin of your thoughts becomes a valuable tool in assessing the quality of them, so you can begin to replace the negative with the positive.

- **Practice tolerating discomfort**: This is one I practice on almost a daily basis in my fitness journey. While working out, I am constantly training my body to go beyond comfort. Doing this conditions me to be aware of where discomfort arises, but not be dictated or deterred by the discomfort. It's the same thing in mental conditioning. Morin says, "Being mentally strong doesn't mean you don't experience emotions. In fact, mental strength requires you to become acutely aware of your emotions so you can make the best choice about how to respond. Mental strength is about accepting your feelings without being controlled by them."[19] Many people say they want to grow in their mental toughness but never stretch themselves past the current version of themselves. In order to be something more, we have to push ourselves to step into something more. "We must step into the unrealized version of ourselves to practice living in this unfamiliar place until it becomes normal."

■ **Reflect on your progress daily:** The simplicity yet powerfulness of this principle is packed with potential. We must slow down in order to assess and reflect on what we are working on so that we can evaluate our progress. Many of us are growing but don't realize it, because we never take a moment to reflect on how far we've come. Taking time to reflect and ponder on how you've faired in your goals is critical. The creation of margin to review what you've done while looking at what it's going to take to get where you're going is a major key to growing your mental strength!

INTERPERSONAL STRENGTH

What does it mean to have interpersonal strength? To understand what it means, you must grasp the concept of interpersonal skills. Interpersonal skills are the behaviors and tactics a person uses to interact with others effectively. In the business world, the term refers to an employee's ability to work well with others.[20] I believe interpersonal skills are some of the most underdeveloped yet critical skills in most people. What is often not realized is that how you interact with people can propel you forward or set you back. This is important, because if you're truly going to become LeaderFit, you must place an emphasis on the strength, or the lack of strength, in this area.

There is a fundamental exercise we all must do in order to build our interpersonal strength. Like in any area we want to see progress, we must assess our current state. One way we can assess our state of interpersonal strength is by asking a series of questions:

- Do people enjoy being around me, or do they tolerate me?
- As a leader, does the quantity of relational equity I have with those I lead depend on what I can do for them or who I am to them?
- If I wasn't an established leader in my organization or circle of influence, what would the quality of my relationships be?
- Would I truly have relationships if I wasn't controlling the terms of the relationship?

Some would say these are harsh questions, but I would say they are necessary questions. If we don't take an honest, unfiltered assessment of how our relationships are set up, we will never be able to see where we need to make adjustments. Just like we can increase our physical and mental capacity, we can grow in our interpersonal capacity. I believe we should all look to grow interpersonally, because a great sign of your leadership effectiveness is if people really want to be around you when they are not required to be. Do people tolerate you, or do they gravitate to you?

If you can't answer those questions along with the others that were posed earlier with confidence and assurance, then it's time to go to work. One of the major ways you can grow in your interpersonal strength involves something that most people don't like to engage in. I'm talking about intentionally becoming vulnerable with those around you. In order to grow interpersonally, you have to practice vulnerability. You must begin asking people their unfiltered feedback about how you are to be around and work with. This may be tough, because you also have to assure those you engage in this process that there will be no retaliation if you don't like what they say about you. This could be very difficult, but I believe it is a critical step in growing in interpersonal strength.

As I've shared some keys to growing in our spiritual, physical, mental, and interpersonal strength, I want to give an easy-to-remember guide to being strong. All of the things I've shared in this chapter are critical to being LeaderFit, however, it doesn't end there. We have to take those attributes and combine them with what may seem like intangible qualities, outlooks, and skills.

For me, the "STRONG" who survive the myriad of crises, challenges, and successes of life are as follows:

1] **Sensible:** They are reasonable and rational in how they see the world and themselves. Sober-minded about what it takes to be productive, they don't think too highly of themselves.

2] **Teachable:** They have child-like curiosity and have left their ego at the door. They are not too prideful to say, "I don't know," and they are always looking to see how they can grow and learn.

3] **Reachable:** They are available to do the work and receive the constructive correction when needed. This person is not self-centered. They are always opening their arms to ask if there is anything they can do to serve you and are never too busy to help someone else accomplish their goals.

4] **Opportunistic:** They aren't afraid to pioneer, go where no one has gone before, and create what isn't yet in existence. Being opportunistic often gets a bad rap. In this case, an opportunistic person is always looking for the winning edge.

5] **Nuanced:** They have to have the ability to see the subtle distinctions and differences that are readily noticed. For example, in fitness, I have to notice the difference not only in weight, but also in outcomes in having my expecting wife lift 8lb dumbbells in doing her squat curls vs. her usual 15lb dumbbells for two sets of 20. What she could do in one season is not permissible for the current season.

6] **Generous:** They understand the power of "give, and it shall be given unto you." A generous person understands that everything they give out is never lost but is a seed that produces a harvest.

The statement "The Strong Survive" is packed with more meaning than an outward show of strength. As one who is LeaderFit, it means developing a full body of work. Being strong is often perceived in a myopic fashion, but we now see that is not accurate. To be strong means that you are not satisfied with the status quo. You are constantly growing and shaping yourself in order to be the best version of yourself.

My question is: Are you strong? If you're not, what can you do today to get strong?

CHAPTER 6:

MUSCLE MEMORY

"Things done out of habit without thought for the future can become a trap door of commonality, complacency, and corrosion."
–DR. KENDRA A. MOMON

One of the hardest things to do in life is "retrain the brain." The research suggests that a new habit can be created in 15-28 days. However, I'm not altogether convinced that less than 30 days of "new thinking" really releases and renews what can be 30 years of "stinking thinking" and holding patterns of behaviors that have now become a part of our muscle memory.

Think about it. How many times do you have to make a stop at a store before you go home? it's been a long day, you're tired, and you're just starting to drive. Before you know it, you're headed home when you actually need to be headed in the opposite direction. I don't know about you, but muscle memory has caused me to do this more times than I'd like to admit.

I share this to say that from a LeaderFit perspective, we have to be willing to step outside the comforts of complacency and "lean into" the possibilities of "behold, I make all things new," God offers "new mercies every morning," and "goodness and mercy will follow you all the days of your life."

What am I getting at? LeaderFit is both a spiritual discipline and mindset. I reiterate: LeaderFit is both a spiritual discipline and mindset. One of the most dangerous things we can do as leaders is to have the mindset or posture of "I already know that," or, "This is the way it's always been done and will continue to be done."

If you are reading this and realize you think those thoughts, I want to challenge you to shift your perspective, because you could very well be on the verge of making yourself obsolete. As leaders, each and every one of us have to choose to challenge our norms for the sake of future growth.

The Merriam-Webster Dictionary defines muscle memory as the ability to repeat a specific muscular movement with improved efficiency and accuracy that is acquired through practice and repetition.[21]

While muscle memory can be a good thing when it comes to reinforcing positive attributes or skills, the principle also can work in a negative direction. If you grew up anything like me, you have heard the adage, "Practice makes perfect." This statement is drilled into the heads of children, athletes, and pretty much anyone who is trying to improve their competency in a particular area. The challenge with this statement is that it's not fully accurate. It would be more accurate to say, "Practice makes permanent."

I remember being challenged with this statement by my childhood tennis coach, Coach Rush, while living in Milwaukee, Wisconsin. I can remember him saying, "Son," he called everybody son. "It's not enough to just practice. You have to practice the right way, because practice doesn't make perfect; practice makes permanent."

From a young age, I realized that it wasn't enough to exercise repetition alone; you must repeat things in the correct manner if you want to truly see progress. This is critical to understand, or you will find yourself locking into habits that are not fruitful and take years to unlearn.

The LeaderFit journey calls for people who are flexible, teachable, and open to build muscle memory that will reinforce beneficial attributes in their lives. As a matter of fact, you have to be willing to be a re-learner for the sake of your future.

There is a powerful quote by American writer Alvin Toffler, who was known as a futurist. He said, "The illiterate of the 21st century will not be those who cannot read or write, but those who cannot learn, unlearn, and relearn."[22]

This principle is powerful in every way. In order to remain relevant and effective, you have to be a person who is committed to changing. That may sound odd, but if you are committed to change, you are committed to maintaining flexibility to relearn over and over again.

As I stated, LeaderFit is both a spiritual discipline and a mindset. One of the ways that I keep myself in the posture of being a re-learner is by ensuring that I position myself not just in my physical approach to life, but also in my spiritual life. Before I ever lift any weights, or do any cardio, I spend time in the presence of the Lord, preparing my heart and mind for the day and offering up this flesh of mine to God the Father. I understand that in order for me to move throughout the day in the most optimal way, I must commit the fullness of my day to the Lord. This is the key that unlocks my ability to lead and live at a high level.

I'm often asked how I balance the different professional responsibilities that I have while still staying in shape and maintaining my overall fitness. My answer is simple. I recognize that without taking the time to submit my thoughts, my intentions, and my planned actions to the Lord, I would be reinforcing a spiritual muscle of self-preservation and self-reliance.

One of my life scriptures is Galatians 2:20. "I have been crucified with Christ [that is, in Him I have shared His crucifixion]; it is no longer I who live, but Christ lives in me. The life I now live in the body I live by faith [by adhering to, relying on, and completely trusting] in the Son of God, who loved me and gave Himself up for me" (The Amplified Bible).

This scripture speaks so loudly to me and represents the essence of how I approach my days. When I read and confess this scripture as I start my days, it reminds me of the heart posture I need to embody daily. Let me show you how I process this as a way of guiding my life: I use this scripture to set my mind and spirit in a posture to re-learn daily and yield to God's purpose over mine, creating new spiritual, mental, emotional, and even psychological muscle memory.

In saying I am crucified with Christ, I'm yielding myself to God's will as Jesus did in His crucifixion. Like Jesus, I choose to sacrifice my will for God's, so that the plan of God can be realized in my life. In no way can I compare with the physical pain and agony Jesus experienced when He voluntarily died on the cross for our sins. I can, however, follow His example of giving Himself up for God's greater plan as He sacrificed His immediate comfort to please God the Father.

As I daily take on this heart posture, I am reminding myself that it's not about what's important to me. It's about what's important to God and how the life I exemplify should reflect that. The most important part of this approach is that I am practicing the exercise of reliance on God over my own ability and intentionally putting my trust in God over myself. To do this daily takes intentionality and discipline, because it's easy to begin to rely on yourself and your ability. Self-reliance is often glorified in our society, but I know that attempting to walk this journey of life without reliance on God is self-sabotage.

I want to give a very clear reality check when it comes to re-learning in the manner I'm describing here. For some, this concept of willingly crucifying your desire and will for the sake of God's plan may sound very noble. For others, it may seem very hard and maybe even impossible. I want to be clear that re-learning and re-directing from where you take your cues on how you live your life can be a tough thing. We are talking about a total mind-shift. It is a true building up of new life skills—mental and spiritual muscles that could seem like an extreme exception to your normal operation.

Just like it takes extreme discipline and focus to see results in your physical fitness, it will take that same, if not more, discipline and focus to see results in the area of your spiritual commitment. To build new muscles in your leadership, fitness, and mindset, we must all undergo a process of renovating. In order to be LeaderFit, we must take the initiative to voluntarily put ourselves in position to clearly see what is present in our lives that needs to stay and go.

The challenge that arises regards the measure by which are we judging what needs to stay and go. We often judge the validity and necessity of a particular way of doing things by what everyone else is doing or by what's popular in culture. When this happens, you settle for comfort, and you may even experience some level of success. But this pales in comparison with God's desire to stretch you to your potential and for you to experience true significance.

Building new muscle memory is not a process of comfort. You must approach the task at hand with committed resilience to what could be a very unfamiliar and possibly intimidating exercise. This approach to life keeps you uncomfortable. It lends to you becoming a person who is always looking to change for the better instead of settling for what is generally and socially accepted.

To build new mental, spiritual, and physical muscle memory, we have to take ourselves through a process of tearing down or alleviating the former accepted foundation in order to build a new one. I want to be very clear and say that this process of putting yourself in position to release old ways can be tough, especially when you are operating based on a reality that has seemingly worked for all of your life.

Scripturally, we see in Romans 12 that the Apostle Paul literally begs the believers in Rome to consider another way than continuing with the way they had been operating. Rome was synonymous with power, influence, and control. I can imagine that there were a lot of people who called themselves leaders in that day that lived with a posture of confidence in their own ability. This is why this hallmark scripture is that much more powerful. Paul says in Romans 12:1-2:

> Therefore, I urge you, brothers and sisters, in view of God's mercy, to offer your bodies as a living sacrifice, holy and pleasing to God—this is your true and proper worship. Do not conform to the pattern of this world, but be transformed by the renewing of your mind. Then you will be able to test and approve what God's will is—his good, pleasing and perfect will" (NIV).

I sense that Paul is trying hard to tell the people of Rome that there is a better way to live. As he communicates this, he is admonishing them against falling into the status quo of what everyone else was doing and how they were living. The key to ensuring they didn't fall into the trap of popular association was undergoing a mind renovation. He is saying that they would have to go through a total shift of how they thought by tearing down their present models of life and rebuilding them with new insight from God. The renovation of the mind is necessary to live a life that meets God's standards.

The new formation of muscle memory I've been alluding to this entire chapter is the formation of a disciplined way of living that enables you to build habits in your life that lead to God-pleasing results. Once you've conditioned yourself to operate this way, you'll find that you will begin to live a life that others will want to emulate.

While it's great that people will see something in you worth modeling themselves after, they must understand that they will need to undergo their own personal rigors of discipline to attain similar results. I am often asked about my formula for effectiveness when it comes to executing life at a high level. My answer, time and time again, is summed up in one word—consistency!

Many times, that answer is not enough for people. They want tactics and specifics. They want to know how long it will take and how hard will it be. I answer again, "It's all about consistency." I've noticed that many people would prefer a quick fix that involves them going extremely hard at something for short periods of time instead of conditioning themselves to do something consistently over a long period of time.

Here is what I say to that: Building muscle memory is not about intensity, it is about consistency! To be a person who is LeaderFit, you can't expect to gain anything worthwhile in a single moment. You must be willing to condition, re-condition, and re-learn if you want long-term results.

I'm currently seeing this in my life. I am juggling multiple responsibilities, and it could be easy for me to think that since my time is more limited, I'll need to adjust how many times a week I'll workout. What

I have decided is that my long-term health is more important than short-term comfort!

Time and time again, when people get busy in life, the first thing they cut from their schedules is their fitness regimen. It's not the social lunches and dinners. It's not the time they use for entertainment, like the movies or sports. It is a person's commitment to fitness that often takes the hit. I've discovered that it's more beneficial to adjust the time you spend at the gym over simply not going to the gym at all. Going to the gym for 25 to 30 minutes a day, five days a week beats only going two days a week and trying to kill yourself in a two-hour workout. When you consistently go for shorter amounts of time, you're training your body to make physical exercise the norm rather than the exception. You're also training your mind that you will be consistent and committed to goals no matter how circumstances change.

Life will be full of different seasons that require adjustments in how you approach them. When you train yourself to be consistent, you are training yourself to win no matter the season! As a leader who trains themselves to live with consistency, it will become more and more evident that you are modeling a lifestyle that people will find worth following. I say this because there are many people looking for a blueprint to follow. They are looking for someone who will confidently say what they believe, and more importantly, do what they say they believed. The challenge is that often, those who have been looked at to model standards of excellence have found it hard to truly be consistent. It is a burden of mine to live a life that gives people an example of a standard that may not be easy, but is consistent. It's only because of my choice to submit to daily spiritual disciplines and healthy mindset mentalities that I am able to offer up anything to others that they can choose to model.

One of the keys to developing LeaderFit muscle memory is mastering the three comforts: commonality, complacency, and corrosion. Each one of these three c's serve as inhibitors you want to avoid in your leadership and fitness journey. These c's will also aid in effectively building leadership muscles that benefit you for the long run.

COMMONALITY: POSSESSION OF COMMON FEATURES.

This is the temptation to be like everyone else for the sake of remaining comfortable while hiding out in mediocrity. In developing new leadership muscles, it will force you to stand out and put you at risk of criticism for your commitment to excellence. Do you want to be common, or do you want to be a conqueror of your goals?

COMPLACENCY: SELF-SATISFACTION, ESPECIALLY WHEN ACCOMPANIED BY UNAWARENESS OF ACTUAL DANGERS OR DEFICIENCIES.

This is the temptation to be OK with just being OK. The danger in living in the comfort zone is that you never realize what could have been your potential because of a lack of effort. Where there is no challenge, there can be no achievement of anything great. Many people will not challenge themselves for fear of exposing a place they need to grow. When you don't grow, you become obsolete.

CORROSION: TO WEAKEN OR DESTROY GRADUALLY.

This is when the potential of a person withers away because of lack of care for the process of intentional growth—the eating away of life because of fear. It is the gradual destruction resulting from inactivity and lack of attention to opportunities of growth. In leadership, you are either progressing or regressing.

I said earlier that we have to be willing to step outside of the comforts of complacency and "lean into" the possibilities of "behold, I make all things new." Are you willing to re-learn, build new habits, and retrain the brain to lead with a new model of leadership? If you're willing to do so, you will see a ripple effect in your sphere of influence and see your leadership go to a new level.

CHAPTER 7:

FOLLOW THE LEADER: ARE YOU LEADING OTHERS TO LIFE OR DEATH?

"Leadership is lifting a person's vision to higher sights, the raising of a person's performance to a higher standard, the building of a personality beyond its normal limitations."[23]
–PETER DRUCKER

Not a week goes by that I don't have someone send me a direct message on Instagram or a text message asking, "Can I workout with you sometime?" If it's not someone asking to workout at the gym with me, it's a request to have coffee or lunch to discuss questions they may have about their calling and purpose in life. When I see these requests come through, I always pause to reflect on what I believe is the main reason a person would reach out and ask this of me. In doing so, a great sense of humility consistently comes over me, understanding that someone recognizes something of enough value in me that they would want to enter my world to glean something that piqued their interest.

After I've processed what an honor it is that someone is inspired by my lifestyle, my mind quickly shifts to another emotion. I start to feel a weight come upon me, something I call the burden of leadership responsibility. The burden of leadership responsibility is the understanding that your actions affect more than you. While it's humbling that someone would want to follow your lead, there is real responsibility that comes with it.

Several people say they want to be a leader and get excited about the idea of doing so. I, however, have always thought about the ramifications of leadership more than coveting the position of leadership. What all people who aspire to lead must grasp is that leadership is a burden of responsibility that many have not proven strong enough to carry effectively because they have not properly counted the cost of leadership.

Another major thing to consider when it comes to assuming the coveted titled of leader is that your level of accountability changes immediately. You are now held to a higher standard. You are saying to God and the people you lead that you acknowledge that your life not only reflects you, but those you suppose leadership over.

The Bible warns us to not be those who covet the position of leadership. We should most especially not desire leadership without counting the cost. James 3:1 says, "My dear brothers and sisters, don't be so eager to become a teacher in the church since you know that we who teach are held to a higher standard of judgment" (The Passion Translation).

The scripture speaks to those who desire to teach, which I believe directly correlates with what a leader should be. A leader should not be one who only dictates and points out directions or tasks; a true leader is one who knows the way, shows the way, and goes out of their way to ensure that those who are following them become equipped to encounter a new way.

When this happens, a true leader walks in a sense of security and can get out of the way. While this scripture speaks directly to the ramifications of aspiring to be a leader in the church, I believe this applies in all areas of life. The fact that we who lead are looked to as trusted guides through the pathways of life should place godly fear in our hearts.

It is a passion of mine to see people grow as leaders. One of the most fulfilling things for me to do is take time answering questions from an aspiring or developing leader to see them reach their potential. I often tell those who desire my mentorship that I'm willing to pour as much as they are willing to receive. I don't force my agenda or philosophy of life on them, but if they want to glean from me, I'm more than willing to share what I have. I am constantly on the lookout for those who want to become LeaderFit.

To take on the essence of becoming LeaderFit, you must live in a posture of always learning while always giving. If you are currently an established leader in your organization, church, business, or family, you must remain teachable while leading. I believe that every leader must figuratively take on the posture of a funnel. This means you are always open to taking in knowledge and wisdom as you glean from someone you respect as a leader. At the same time, you are always open to allowing what you are learning to be shared with those who respect you as a leader.

Your ability to develop leaders is a sign that you are LeaderFit. As a leader, I think we all have to be vulnerable enough to ask: Am I a leader worth following, and if so, what do I need to do to effectively develop more leaders? What if I told you that the measure of your leadership is not in what you accomplish but in the quality of the leaders you develop? I love this quote by Derwin Gray, as he captures my sentiments around leadership development very well: "The best leaders look into the soul of a person and say, I see what you could be, and my role is to bring that out of you."[24]

I want to walk us through some of the principles and concepts that I think are critical:

- You are what you model before others.
  - We must all realize that someone is always watching. "People always listen to what you say with your actions more than that what they hear with your words."
- Most followers are mimicking the model.
  - Be mindful of your model. If your model of leadership is fractured, that's what you'll reproduce. We reproduce what we are, not what we hope to be.
- What model are you following?
  - Is your leadership model Christ-based and principle-centered? You don't want to model your leadership model based on a human standard, but rather Christ's standard. These types of leaders can take longer to unearth but are easily replicated after.

When it comes to developing leaders today, it takes commitment. It is not enough to simply have blind loyalty to your way of doing things, especially if you want to see any real buy-in and opportunity to equip your leaders to lead beyond you. Here are a few things to consider as you exercise your leadership development:

- **Clearly identify what you want to model:** Identify what the goal is and how you will accomplish it. I've seen far too many models that are filled with ambiguity where the standard is not clearly communicated. In this case, the measuring line is always moving, and there's no clear gauge on the effectiveness of the development process. When you clarify your desire, you can more effectively hold people accountable.

- **Give the why**: Be OK with explaining the why behind the what. Be willing to do if often if you want to see healthy leaders grow. When you take time to teach the why, your future issues become easier to solve, because more people are equipped with the wisdom to handle challenges.

- **Be patient**: If you spend the time at the beginning, you'll build effective, sustainable leaders for the long run. Settle in your heart that you must be responsible for equipping and pre-paring your bench of leaders. The future of your leadership effectiveness lies in your ability to patiently develop now. Don't expect the team that surrounds you to come in fully developed.

If you can follow these tips, I am confident that you will see a positive return on your investment into your teams, as all leaders need to be receiving and giving in the area of leadership growth and develop-ment. Without positioning yourself to grow, you are setting yourself up to become obsolete.

While you're looking to lead and develop others, here are some things to consider in order to take the next step in your LeaderFitness.

Take a moment to answer these questions:

1] **Who am I becoming?** (A question of growth.)

List two things you are actively doing to have a marked difference in the before and after of when you started your leadership journey versus when you've had a more established tenure in leadership.

2] **What do I need to change?** (A question of reevaluation.)

List two things to change or two new habits to form. You should ask, "Am I yielding the type of results and progress that I should be based on the mental, emotional, and spiritual energy I'm exerting while leading?"

3] **Who will I bring with me?** (A question of care.)

Select one person that you commit to connecting with, and be accountable in helping lift them in an area they may be struggling in. Remember that the gauge of your leadership is measured by the quality of leaders you develop under your watch. It takes care and intentionality to pour into another potential leader who may not have started their leadership journey in the same way as you. You may be wondering about some practical ways to intentionally develop people in their leadership journey. The sober reality is that it takes time to develop leaders, but it can be done. It is a process in which you have to invest time, teaching, watching, coaching, and then releasing.

A great book concerning the process of developing leaders is *Hero Maker*. Dave Ferguson, the author, walks us through how we can take an emerging leader and guide them through levels of growth in order for them to be equipped to lead on their own. Here are some quick tips I learned about developing leaders from the book:[25]

- **Level 1:** Watch what I do, and then let's talk about it.
- **Level 2:** Let's together figure out a plan for what you should do.
- **Level 3:** Propose a plan for what I should do, and let's talk about it.
- **Level 4:** Let me know your plan for what you should do, but wait for my feedback.
- **Level 5:** You should handle it completely, and then let me know what you did.
- **Level 6:** You should handle it completely, and there is no need to report back to me.

SPIRITUAL SPOTTERS

This process that we've discussed is an approach to life that you can't do on your own. The entire philosophy of leadership growth is something that is directly tied to the involvement of at least one other person. This is important to note, because many people attempt to attack the journey of growth alone. It is my belief that every individual must make a determination in his or her heart that he or she want to grow before any part of the growth process can start. The key to growth being realized, however, does not rest solely on that inward desire. Each one of us is going to have to involve others to see intentional and measurable progress.

I can hear the independent soul reading this, saying, "I don't need anyone else in order for me to grow."

I beg to differ. I have learned a very helpful and critical principle throughout both my leadership and fitness journey. I've come to realize that while I am extremely determined and disciplined within myself, there is only so far I can go and so much I can grow by myself!

There are times when I'm working out, and I'm attempting to lift a particular amount of weight that's beyond my current ability. During these very uncomfortable and strenuous times, I need something more than willpower. The thing I need is actually someone to assist me in lifting the weight I'm under so that it doesn't injure me. The term for this person is called a spotter. The Merriam-Webster Dictionary defines a spotter as a person who assists during exercise to help prevent injury.[26] Someone who keeps watch. It is even defined as one who locates enemy targets. While having someone spot you at the gym when you're pushing your limits is important, it is even more important that you have someone in your leadership and personal development life serve as a spotter. I call these individuals "Spiritual Spotters."

A spiritual spotter is someone you can count on to be there to help guide you through your journey of growth. They will not lift the weight of life for you, but they will partner with you to encourage you physically, emotionally, and spiritually. These are people who are encouragers, accountability partners, and those you look to you for inspiration.

I have a few spiritual spotters in my life. My wife, Kendra, serves as my primary and most critical spiritual spotter. She is always there for me to encourage me, to offer perspectives on things that I don't see, and ultimately to look out for my best interests at all times. I would have been crushed under the weight of life several times over if I didn't have her as my primary spiritual spotter.

I have great friends like Darius Wise, whom I've known for over 20 years. Because of the tenure of our relationship, he is able to challenge me and even pick up on areas where I may be taking it too easy and becoming complacent. He is able to recognize when I need a jolt of inspiration, as well as when I need correction.

A spiritual spotter is someone who sees your potential and wants to see you grow. They care enough about you to not completely alleviate the weight of life from you, but to be there as a support as you press through on your way to growth. I want to encourage you to list at least one spiritual spotter. My challenge for you is to not only nurture the relationship with that one person, but also set a goal to find a total of three. Also, be sure that you are availing yourself to be a spiritual spotter to someone else. As I've said many times in this chapter, a person who is LeaderFit is always receiving leadership for their growth, while at the same time, giving out leadership to others.

SPIRITUAL SPOTTERS:

1] _____

2] _____

3] _____

CHAPTER 8:

EMOTIONAL FITNESS

*"The body has been designed to renew itself through
continuous self-correction. These same principles also
apply to the healing of psyche, spirit, and soul."*[27]
–PETER A. LEVINE

I recently ministered a word on healing and forgiveness where I spoke about owing nothing to another, but instead loving them. I talked about how many times, we are told to "faith it until we make it," yet years later, we are trapped by the scar tissue of pain, trauma, and abuse that we suppressed, didn't acknowledge, and unfortunately are still dealing with emotionally. I shared what my wife always says, "Reveal it, so Jesus can heal it!"

In reflecting on the importance and preserving power of emotional health, I couldn't write this book on leader fitness without emphasizing the importance of emotional health. I want to take this a step further and say that I advocate emotional health over physical health! If we are truly going to be LeaderFit, we must first choose to become emotionally healthy and embrace all of the life-giving and sustaining benefits associated with this area of health.

3 John 1:2 captures this so well, "Beloved, I pray that you may prosper in all things and be healthy, even as your soul prospers" (The World English Bible).

Let me frame it this way: Leader fitness is a one-two combo that is essential to our overall wellness and soul care. I'm not telling you something I read about, I'm telling you what I know from my lived experiences. I know from experiencing one of the most painful caves that with the help and guidance of God, my therapist, and some of my closest friends who served as my spiritual spotters, I was able to crawl out of healthy and whole.

Read that again. Even I needed more than my faith in God when my soul was unexpectedly shipwrecked. I needed the help of God, my counselor, and my spiritual spotters. I also had to choose to rely on spiritual and leadership disciplines developed over time that had become a part of my daily routine. In particular, I had to choose to spend time in prayer and meditation, read the Word of God, get filled by the Word, engage in small group fellowship, and be vulnerable to a few trusted leaders and mentors on my good days and even on my most debilitating days.

Without going into all of the details, the emotional shipwrecking I experienced was the dissolution of my first marriage. As a young man who rededicated my life to the Lord at 17, I engaged in a radical transformation process where I went from being nominated "most likely to tear up the club every weekend" by my high school senior classmates, to becoming a two-sport campus leader and minister for Fellowship of Christian Athletes.

Imagine a Friday night that while my teammates are having a ball, I am in my dorm room praying, leading a Bible study, or walking a peer through the ABC's of salvation. I share this by way of background, because one of the things I desired above all other things was to one day marry and start a family. At 24 years of age, in front of God, my pastor, and others, I actualized one of the desires of my heart and got married. Four years later, when the marriage was beyond the point of repair, I was devastated not only by this private loss, but also the public pain associated with it.

Here I was, recently single, processing the pain and regret of it all, watching as my friends are starting and growing their families, living their best lives, and life is seemingly passing me by. I remember the times when the emotional pain was so overwhelming that I had to take something to go to sleep at night, and then I had to take some-thing else to get me going in the morning. I remember the day my best friend, in an effort to try to empathize with me, said, "Man, I feel you. I understand. I got you!"

To this day, I also remember what I said back to him. In a moment of clarity and honesty, I said, "No, you don't! You are still married with a beautiful wife and family. You don't know this kind of pain, bro!"

I share this story because it was a crucial moment in our decade-plus friendship. While my response was hard for my bro to hear, he never left my side, walking with me, spotting for me, praying for me, and encouraging me throughout my journey toward emotional health and healing.

More than a decade later, and by the grace of God, I am on the other side of this emotional pain and trauma which I now know was designed to hinder me. What I can see clearly now is that while I didn't lose my physical disciplines, I would have surely lost my emotional and, ultimately, my spiritual disciplines if I hadn't made the decision to walk through the necessary processes of emotional healing and health.

What is the takeaway from all of this? I champion emotional health just as much, if not more, than I champion physical health. I also know that God is a healer, restorer, and remembers the greatest desires of heart. Today, I am happily married to my wife, Kendra, who is a dynamic woman, leader, mentor, and friend to many. We are expecting our first son, Maximus, and I am walking in my purpose, calling, and destiny, fulfilled, grateful, and passionate about helping others do the same.

I don't share this to brag. I share this as an encouragement to anyone currently in an emotional pit. I want you to know there is true joy for our mourning and beauty for our ashes awaiting us. I also want to share a few of the crystalizing lessons I learned from my personal journey of emotional healing.

LESSON 1: INVITE GOD INTO YOUR EMOTIONS

So simple, right? In theory, it seems like a no-brainer. In practice, however, it's not as easy as it seems. For strong-willed, self-reliant, or self-made individuals in particular, this can be a hard and humbling thing to do. It can also be difficult to invite God into your emotions if you didn't grow up with a well-rounded perspective or understanding of God as Abba, our loving Father. By inviting God into our emotions, we begin the process of intentional vulnerability and transparency where we acknowledge that what we need goes beyond what we can see or even do for ourselves. We also acknowledge that He holds it all together and partake in the beautiful exchange of "casting our cares on Him because He cares for us."

LESSON 2: ACKNOWLEDGE YOUR EMOTIONS

One of the greatest lies I've seen perpetuated in both ministry and the marketplace is the false narrative of feelings not mattering. Taking it all the way back to childhood, we were taught and told to lie about or deny our feelings by being told things like:

"Suck it up!"

"Big boys don't cry."

"It's OK."

"They didn't mean it."

"If you don't stop crying, I will give you something to cry about."

You get the drift. You can insert you own false narrative in here, and it all amounts to the same thing. So many of us were denied safe spaces to process our emotions as children, teens, and even adults. As a result, we have trained our brain to either stuff, suppress, or ignore our emotions and feelings.

Say this out loud: "My emotions and feelings are real. It is OK to acknowledge that I am hurt, disappointed, angry, or feeling shame. While my feelings are real, I acknowledge that God can heal. I invite

Him into these hurting places and will let His love, not my emotions, reveal the areas I need to embrace healing."

In addition to going through the spiritual aspects of healing, I also strongly recommend seeking out and aligning with professional counselors, trauma care specialists, and mental health advocates who are equipped and trained to provide expert care and counseling. Let me put it this way: I believe in both the healing power of God and the professional help of counselors, psychologists, psychiatrists, trauma care specialists, behavioral, and neurological experts.

Lastly, I personally advocate plugging into a safe space of community through small groups, prayer groups, common interest groups, and the like. Community can also consist of health friends, family, and colleagues who are pointing you toward health, wholeness, and accountability.

LESSON 3: BEGIN AGAIN

One of my favorite books is *The Four Agreements: A Practical Guide to Personal Freedom* by Don Miguel Ruiz. The book is a code of ethics and conduct based on Toltec wisdom. The agreements are as follows:

1] Be Impeccable with Your Word
2] Don't Take Anything Personally
3] Don't Make Assumptions
4] Do Your Best[28]

I share these agreements because I've noticed that when we are going through emotional challenges and crises, it can be hard to remember these agreements. Often, we can take on a victim or woe-is-me mentality where it is easy to get stuck in the doldrums of, "I don't deserve this," or, "This shouldn't have happened to me."

In committing to begin again, I am able to get back up, clothed in fresh perspective, knowing no matter how much it hurts or what other people do or say about me, even the negative actions expressed toward me really have nothing to do with me. Regardless of how I feel, I will speak life over myself and be impeccable with my words to create life-giving and sustaining thoughts, not negative, condemning, self-hating or defeating thoughts.

In committing to begin again, I will remain committed to not taking anything personally, and I also won't make assumptions about why someone did or said something negative to me or about me. Lastly, on my good days, bad days, indifferent days, and even painful days, I will commit to doing my best to keep going, keep growing, and continue on my healing journey toward freedom, life, and leader fitness.

CHAPTER 9:

FAMILY FITNESS

We've all heard the saying, "A family that prays together, stays together." I am a firm believer in this. As a matter of fact, about a year ago, I had this compelling conviction to connect with my wife every single day and pray for each other. While we have consistently prayed together throughout our marriage and have our own personal prayer times, we had never connected to pray every single day. Now, before you get all in your feelings that we established are real in the last chapter, let me help you out. While Kendra and I connect every day to pray, it's not the length or amount of time spent in prayer that has made a difference. It's been the commitment to consistency in prioritizing our family's spiritual wellness and fitness that has been the secret weapon in our intentional time of prayer.

Truth be told, our prayer time isn't always long. The fruit of these times of covering, however, is always strong in our lives. As a matter of fact, I love when she shares the story of the first time I prayed for her before she had a speaking engagement. At the time, we were "interested" in each other, but were committed to navigating as friends. When I took her hands in mine, she shared that she couldn't focus on what I was praying, because she was praying, "I don't like this guy. Jesus, help me to not like this man. Oh, Lord, I can't like this guy." I still laugh about this double-minded prayer, but don't lose the point. Our initial connection in prayer remains a cornerstone that we had to be intentional about preserving in our lives.

I share this because we had to make an intentional decision to incorporate the spiritual discipline of corporate prayer into our family life so that we didn't unintentionally allow the pace of our lives to dictate and overtake the foundational pillars, non-negotiables, and spiritual disciplines—the sustainers of our life. Prayer has always been a fundamental part of our connection, marriage, and life and remain so for the rest of our lives.

There are a few other things that shape our family fitness values. These are our family core values that shape, navigate, and define our why. They are core values in that they represent our gravitational center, inner strength, and centrality of our family.

OUR FIRST FAMILY FITNESS CORE VALUE IS LOVE.

Kendra and I love to love each other. One of the things I say often is, "I love to love Kendra, and she loves to love me right back!" I want to be clear that this isn't just a cliché saying to try to get brownie points or impress others. I genuinely mean it, feel it, and know how blessed I am to experience authentic love in this lifetime.

Our love is rooted in knowing that God has put us together and that we choose to love, honor, and respect each other daily. We also try to walk out the three forms of love—eros, philia, and agape—by being open, transparent, and vulnerable with each other when we knock it out of the park in speaking each other's love language. When we fail miserably, we try to walk, live, and lead in love first. One of our foundational "MO-ISM's" is the following statement: Remember what I told you in the light when it gets dark.

As shared, I experienced deep emotional hurt, trauma, and disappointment that forced me to begin again. During those dark days, I had to remember who God said I was when I was no longer certain. I remember the impact and impression when I realized that it does matter: the darkness (the trauma, disappointment, hurt, or betrayal), what I spoke over you, said about you, and what others affirmed. When Kendra and I have a disagreement, we never disrespect, disregard, or dismiss each other because of our core commitment to love each other and remember what we said in the light even when it gets a little dark.

OUR SECOND FAMILY FITNESS
CORE VALUE IS HONOR.

One of the things that is becoming an increasingly lost art is the culture of honor. Whether in society, culture, or our personal lives, the cancel culture mentality has caused so many to devalue and dishonor others. For Kendra and me, honor means placing the other person's needs, wants, and desires above our own preferences. It also means being committed to talking through it and hearing each other's hearts when we are at an impasse, because the other person's preferences and priorities are equal to our own.

Honor also means that we never purposefully try to compete with each other, demean each other, or even post things about each other, such as vulnerable or unflattering pictures of each other as a means of joking, clapping back, or exacting revenge. We share these things even when we do premarital counseling, because we want everyone to know that if we are going to become LeaderFit in our marriages and families, we must be committed to our calling to love and cover, not expose or uncover each other!

OUR THIRD FAMILY FITNESS
CORE VALUE IS RESPECT.

It's simple. We choose to respect each other, which means we esteem, regard, and think highly of one another even when we don't agree. One of the things I share with a lot of guys that God really helped me to process is that I can't want Kendra's talents, skills, and giftings that God has blessed her with when it benefits me, but disregard or be dismissive of her on the days when her wisdom, discernment, articulation, insight, and strong leadership wiring gets on my nerves and rubs me the wrong way. Kendra, who is also the Interim Provost and Vice President of Academic Affairs at Oglethorpe University, also had to learn to yield to me as someone who has always been strong, independent, in charge, and self-reliant. Earlier in our marriage, she had to learn how to take the professor hat off and not inadvertently lecture me on what I "needed" to be doing. I don't know where you are with respecting your spouse on your LeaderFit journey. What I do know is that there is freedom and even greater love for each other in discovering, valuing, and respecting each other.

OUR FOURTH FAMILY CORE VALUE IS A "TWOFER"—TRUST AND TRANSPARENCY.

Trust and transparency are the two foundational pillars our year-long friendship was based on, even before we decided to go public in our dating relationship. We practice both trust and transparency in the small and big things. Whether it's having Life360 on all of our devices, or reminding each other of our personal fitness, financial, or friendship goals, we invite each other into those inner sacred and safe spaces.

OUR FIFTH FAMILY CORE
VALUE IS GENEROSITY.

We try to out-serve, honor, love, give, and do for each other. One of my favorite examples of mutual generosity is in our understanding of cooking and cleaning. How it works is simple: Kendra cooks and I clean. What is even more dynamic about this model is that it's not an immutable absolute. What I mean is that while this is our fundamental mode of operation, I am not exempt from cooking, and she isn't exempt from cleaning the kitchen. As a matter of fact, she recently cooked and cleaned as she knew I was deep in study. When I came out of my office to clean the kitchen, I was blessed by her generous act of kindness toward me.

In the space below, write down your family core values.

_____

_____

_____

_____

_____

The last thing I want to encourage you to do as a steward of your family fitness is to be aware that seasons change. What may have been the focus, highlight, and emphasis of year one of marriage and relationship may not be the focus of year three of marriage and relationship. As such, just like the seasons change, we also must be open to change in our family fitness values. Below are a few things to pay attention to as you navigate this LeaderFit terrain.

1] **Emotional changes:** Pay attention to your response and how you communicate when you are tired, wired, or stressed. One helpful thing to help manage this change is to communicate to your spouse and family as it relates to what you are feeling and where you find yourself.

2] **Relational changes:** Pay attention to when people enter and exit your life. I share that some people are for HIIT (high intensity impact training) seasons of our lives while God sends other people to be a part of the marathons of our lives.

3] **Family changes:** Pay attention to what happens as you go from a single person, to a married couple, to a family with children.

4] **Career changes:** Pay attention to shifts in your professional career, changes in occupational and vocational desires, advancements, promotions, and even relocation opportunities to make sure that your family is bought in and not just going along to get along. Be mindful of the fact that promotion and advancement usually comes with growing pains and stretching. I want to give you some invaluable advice I received. A mentor told me to be open, flexible, and malleable. He said, "Bend and lean into the changes so that what is inevitable doesn't break you!"

5] **Spiritual changes:** Pay attention and take time for personal and family-centered spiritual growth, development, leadership, and discipleship.

As we close out this chapter, I want to share that while these things may seem simple and easy, it will take commitment to continuously put your family values at the forefront and to focus on the why of being LeaderFit in this area of your life.

CHAPTER 10:

LEADERFIT UNLEASHED

We've taken this LeaderFit journey together, and I am so glad you've made it to this point. This final chapter is about taking all of the principles we've discussed and moving them from concept to reality. It's time to move from reading something as a good idea to implementing it into your current state. Your next step should be taking the training wheels off and becoming a doer.

I have a saying that I use when coaching leaders, preaching sermons, or motivating someone at the gym. With extreme intensity, I lean in and say, "There's another you in you!"

It's time to realize your potential. It is time to cut the figurative leash from yourself and begin stepping into new levels of accomplishment, growth, and purpose!

Each and every person should regularly and soberly ask themselves, "Am I really operating at my potential?" If we are honest, most of us don't push ourselves to live out the best version of ourselves every day. Many people are, in some ways, unconsciously saving the energy of their lives for a time when they feel they can fully express and let their true selves out. The challenge with this type of mentality is that the only moments promised to you are the ones you're currently living and breathing in right now! I want to say this as clearly as I can: It is time to stop hiding! It is time to stop the waiting! It is time to unleash the hidden you so that you can realize the true you!

I'm extremely passionate about showing up and realizing your true self, because I went through my own unleashing back in 2009. I had come out of a very difficult season of personal emotional trauma where I started to interrogate myself daily. I would ask myself the following questions, (maybe you can relate):

■ Is this the way you want to exist? Are you living up to your potential? What are the things you've always wanted to do but were afraid to try? What is the worst thing that could happen to you if you try new things? Who do you want to become?

That last question is the one that I believe sparked my unleashing moment. As I wrestled with these questions, I quickly started to realize that there was more for me in life than what I was experiencing. I began to challenge myself to step out of my comfort zone and try things that I would have hesitated on in the past. I realized that people recognized me as being this nice, quiet, introverted, and even at times, passive guy. However, as I began to get more and more comfortable in my own skin, I came to the revelation that I wasn't really that person at all. I made major changes in my life in what seemed like an instant. I moved from a traditional home in the suburbs to a studio apartment right in the middle of Midtown Atlanta. As a kid, I always wanted to study martial arts, so I began taking Muay Thai lessons at a local MMA gym. I transformed from that nice, quiet, introverted, passive version of myself into MOBEAST.

MOBEAST is the version of me that is not afraid to try new things, meet new people, and step out of comfort to experience life in a different way. There are people who knew me before that season of transition, have since come into contact with me, and are shocked. They are shocked that the quiet, unassuming guy who lacked confidence now weekly speaks in front of hundreds and even thousands of people. Some see me today and say, "MO—you've changed." While change is good and has its benefits, I would more accurately say that who I have always had the potential to be was simply trapped on the inside of me.

Being LeaderFit is an unleashing of the dormant qualities of great-ness on the inside of each person. It's not that I became a different person so much as I accepted the way God really intended me to live. I became tired of watching others move into the arena of light-seeing victory while I lived in my proverbial regret. Deep inside, I knew that I had the potential to walk in greatness, but for years, I held myself back because of fear.

I realized that I didn't want to live in regret of not trying to be the best that I could be. What I found was that the more I stretched myself, the more I realized what was possible through me. I have learned so much from simply shifting my mindset from a posture of fear to a true posture of faith. Faith that I could do what I put my mind and heart toward. Faith that if there were goals that matched up with God's purpose in my life, that He would enable me to accomplish them. I realized the sidelines of life were no place for a champion such as myself. I realized I was more than able to do all things through Christ who gives me strength.

One of the major shifts I made was that I began to daily wake up with a YES in my spirit. What I mean by that is that I would start my day with an expectation that circumstances would come into agreement with me for things that were for me. Where a lot of people assume the worst, I stand with a posture where I assume the best. There are some key life lessons I learned during my unleashing season that I believe will benefit you.

PRINCIPLES OF THE POWER
OF UNLEASHING YOU!

1] **Die empty**

Recently, my wife shared how she was prompted by the Lord to "die empty daily." What this means is to start everyday full of purpose and intentionality with an outlook toward what type of deposit you can make in the lives of others. With this in mind, you are not operating in self-preservation mode where you're trying to manage your energy to save it for the next day. The Bible says that we are to pray that God "gives us this day our daily bread." This means that we want God to endow us with what is necessary for this particular day so that we can be fully equipped for the purpose of that day. I don't know who this is for, but if you've been feeling the presence and pressing of the Lord to give more of yourself away, I stand in agreement with you giving him your "YES!"

2] **Don't wait for permission to be!**

Delay is the enemy of progress. We live in a world where there is opportunity all around us daily. When you understand your God-given purpose, you have to fully embrace it and not wait for someone to give you permission to be who God called you to be. If I waited for someone to say "Go Mo! You can do it," I don't even want to think of the life I'd be living right now. I can say it would have be a life of settling. If you've read this far, I don't believe you're a person that wants to settle for less than your full potential.

3] **There is another you in you!**

This is not just a nice cliche or motivational saying. I truly believe that within all of us there a better, more fulfilled, purpose-driven version of ourselves that is waiting to get out. Even if you feel like you're doing very well, I want to challenge you to pray and search yourself for areas where you still might be holding back. In order for us to truly walk in God's full calling for our lives, we have to be willing to risk it all for the sake of meeting God's best version of ourselves. It would be a tragedy to live a long life but not experience the fullness of life. LeaderFit is about conditioning yourself in a way that you max out your life potential.

4] **Finish strong**

So many people say they want to operate in excellence. The challenge with that statement is that the definition of excellence can reside on a sliding scale. For years, I have defined excellence as "a commitment to finishing." A lot of people start well, which is why a lot of the focus of this book is dealing with endurance and conditioning our lives in a way that we can see sustainable results. Your leadership sustainability is often in direct correlation to your leadership endurance. If our LeaderFitness is out of wack, it's indicative of our leadership in a particular area being off track.

As we reflect on these principles of unleashing ourselves, we see there are many factors to consider. I believe they all tie back to some of the questions we posed earlier in the book: What does it mean to be fit? What does fitness really look like? We determined that physical, emotional, psychological, and spiritual fitness, at it's core, is inner health, healing, and wholeness. I love the way my friend Odell Dickerson talks about and sees fitness as it relates to leadership and how he marries the two in his life. I interviewed him for this book. Take a look at what he says:

"To be fit is to live a purposeful life with gratitude, joy, and wholeness. First, to be fit is to be grateful. I am thankful for the level of fitness that God has given me to live a full and purposeful life. I feel like God specifically gave me fitness as a ministry tool to serve Him and as a method of connection in leading (serving). See, my whole life is dedicated to ministry, and ministry is about connecting to people, God's people. Leading simultaneously in ministry and in fitness, my love for fitness directly corresponds with my level of leadership and serves as a witness to others that the impossible can be done. Thus, 'I can do all things through Christ who strengthens me.' I am clear that my 'fitness' comes from God.

"Second, to be fit is to have joy. Fitness brings me joy, and it simultaneously eases the pain that is often caused by life. Scientifically, we know that fitness releases chemicals called endorphins that make you feel good and reduces the perception of pain in the body.

Endorphins are said to trigger positive feelings that are relatable to the feelings of being 'high.' Spiritually, fitness makes me happy, and I know it is God, because God gave it to me. I believe He intended for me to be happy and to have peace.

"Third, to be fit is to be whole. I take a wholistic approach to fitness that includes mind, body, and spirit. I believe there must be synergy, that is, an intentional effort to individually maximize each of these components of fitness at the same time so that they collectively maximize the utilization of one's fitness and ultimately one's life. Aristotle states it this way, 'The whole is greater than the sum of its parts.'"

Fitness impacts my role in leadership by allowing me to show a higher quality of life in serving as well as a higher sense of purpose that requires healthiness and promotes a more fulfilling life. Ultimately, for me, fitness is one powerful way to connect with people, showing them a higher quality of life in aligning with God, because to be fit is to be aligned with God.

Physical fitness improves my leadership by giving me energy, encouragement, and discipline. First, the mind, body, and spirit requires energy, which I define as a currency of strength as well as stamina and endurance that is earned and accumulated through my wholistic approach to fitness training. Once you have earned it, 'you must spend it well and invest in it wisely.'

Second, accomplishments in physical fitness give me a sense of encouragement, which boosts confidence and a desire to do more. In other words, I have made progress, and I can see it 'adding up.' Therefore, I will continue on to accomplish more as leader.

Third, physical fitness develops a discipline that allows you to accomplish things when you are not motivated. Thus, 'You will never always be motivated, so you must learn to be disciplined.'"When I see what people like Odell have to say about the correlation between fitness and leadership, it excites me, because it shows me that I'm not alone in the quest to be the best. It shows me that there are others who want to reach their maximum potential by taking care of themselves in mind, body, and spirit. I believe if more people would approach their life of leadership with a combination of fitness awareness, we would see so many people grow in their effectiveness.

One of my heart's desires is to share the power of being LeaderFit so that those who have accepted the call to lead can lead well and lead for a very long time. This journey must be a combination of the spiritual, mental, physical, and practical for the effects of our leadership to have lasting impact.

As we defined in the first chapter, LeaderFit is "the conditioned ability to positively influence, motivate, equip, and empower others to the achievement of a goal or outcome over a sustained period of time with sustaining impact."

Are you LeaderFit? Are you fit to lead?

Are you conditioned with the ability to reach your goals while helping lead others to accomplish theirs? Are you poised and disciplined enough to not only start the journey of leadership but to commit to finishing your leadership journey strong?

If you now are able to affirmatively answer that question, I'm glad to welcome you into the LeaderFit community!

Let me pray for you as you continue on this journey: Father, in the name of Jesus, I thank you for every reader of this book. I pray that this time we have spent together through the words on these pages has inspired and enlightened Your son or daughter. I'm thankful for what You will do through their lives as they embody the principles in this book to become better leaders. My prayer is that through growing in their LeaderFitness, they will be able to make a lasting deposit in the world around them. I ask that you give them patience, endurance, and discipline to complete the assignment that you've placed in their hearts so that they bring you glory. In Jesus's name, amen.

I'm so excited to hear about the impact you will make as you embody the truths of being LeaderFit!

Let's get it and let's go!

"For physical training is of some value, but godliness has value for all things, holding promise for both the present life and the life to come" (1 Timothy 4:8, NIV).

ENDNOTES

1 https://www.brainyquote.com/quotes/john_c_maxwell_600859. Accessed April 6. 2021.

2 http://psgleadership.scripts.mit.edu/2013IAP/pdf/1_required_reading/ Understanding%20Leadership.pdf. Accessed April 6, 2021.

3 https://www.merriam-webster.com/dictionary/endurance. Accessed April 6, 2021.

4 Monon, Kendra, *Being as Leading: Your Roadmap to Shaping Culture Through Life's Disruptions* (Sanford, FL: Avail, 2020).

5 https://www.goodreads.com/work/quotes/48666706-wealth-for-all-living-a-life-of-success-at-the-edge-of-your-ability. Accessed April 6, 2021.

6 https://www.brainyquote.com/quotes/lao_tzu_137141. Accessed April 6, 2021.

7 Saltos, Gabriela, "MLK, Jr. Asked Us 'What Are You Doing For Others?' Here's How We Answered," *Huffington Post*, January 15, 2015, https://www.huffpost.com/ entry/mlk-day-serving-others_n_6489236.

8 Maxwell, John, *The 21 Irrefutable Laws of Leadership: Follow Them and People Will Follow You* (Nashville: Harper Collins Leadership, 2007).

9 https://www.nasm.org/. Accessed April 6, 2021.

10 https://www.merriam-webster.com/dictionary/discipline. Accessed April 6, 2021.

11 https://truefitness.com/resources/mental-emotional-benefits-exercise/. Accessed April 6, 2021

12 Sanders, Oswald, *Spiritual Leadership* (Chicago: Moody Bible Institute, 1967).

13 https://breakingmuscle.com/fitness/do-you-know-what-your-core-really-is-and-what-it-does. Accessed April 6, 2021.

14 https://dictionary.cambridge.org/us/dictionary/english/value. Accessed April 6, 2021.

15 Maxwell, John, *Change Your World* (Nashville: Harper Collins Leadership, 2021).

16 Lencioni, Patrick. "Make Your Values Mean Something." *Harvard Business Review*, (July, 2002), https://hbr.org/2002/07/make-your-values-mean-something. Accessed April 6, 2021.

17   Henrique, Tim, "Tim's Keys to Building Strength," *All About Powerlifting*. http://allaboutpowerlifting.com/tims-keys-to-building-strength/. Accessed April 6, 2021.

18   Morin, Amy, "5 Powerful Exercises to Increase Your Mental Strength," *Forbes.com*, December 3, 2013, https://www.forbes.com/sites/groupthink/2013/12/03/5-powerful-exercises-to-increase-your-mental-strength/?sh=7dbbb4e04cda. Accessed April 6, 2021.

19   Tim, "Tim's Keys to Building Strength."

20   https://www.investopedia.com/terms/i/interpersonal-skills.asp. Accessed April 6, 2021

21   https://www.merriam-webster.com/dictionary/muscle%20memory. Accessed April 6, 2021.

22   https://usingtechnologybetter.com/a-great-quote-about-learning/. Accessed April 6, 2021.

23   https://www.goodreads.com/quotes/656219-leadership-is-not-magnetic-personality-that-can-just-as-well. Accessed April 6, 2021.

24   Ferguson, Dave, *Hero Maker* (Grand Rapids: Zondervan, 2018).

25   Ferguson, *Hero Maker*

26   https://www.merriam-webster.com/dictionary/spotter. Accessed April 6, 2021.

27   https://www.goodreads.com/work/quotes/374655-waking-the-tiger-healing-trauma. Accessed April 6, 2021.

28   Ruiz, Don Migue, *The Four Agreements: A Practical Guide to Personal Freedom* (San Rafael: Amber-Allen Publishing, Incorporated, 2018).